P9-CLO-239

BOB STEELE:
A MAN AND HIS HUMOR

Illustrated by Bob Steele
Edited by Spoonwood Press

Spoonwood Press
Hartford, Connecticut 1980

Copyright© 1980 by Spoonwood Press
All rights reserved.

First published in 1980 by Spoonwood Press
P.O. Box 3153 Hartford, Connecticut 06103

FIRST EDITION
First printing September 1980
Second printing October 1980

SECOND EDITION
First printing August 1981

Library of Congress Cataloging in Publication Data

Grateful acknowledgement is made to the following for permission to reprint copyrighted material:
   Francis Day & Hunter LTD, 138-140 Charing Cross Road, London WC2H OLD, England
   "The Lion and Albert"© 1933; "The Return of Albert" © 1935.

Photograph Credits. All pictures not otherwise credited are from Bob Steele's private collection.

Printed in the United States of America

CONTENTS

ELLA GRASSO
GOVERNOR

STATE OF CONNECTICUT
EXECUTIVE CHAMBERS
HARTFORD

June, 1980

Long ago and far away, it was observed that, "Mirth resting on earnestness and sadness, as the rainbow on black tempest: only a right valiant heart is capable of that."

For more than four decades, the right valiant heart of one Robert L. Steele (the "L" is for Elmer) has painted a bright rainbow of mirth for listeners far and wide throughout Southern New England. His educated wit and keen insights have brightened our mornings as we sought the strength to face a new day. His puns have strained our imagination. His commitment to the daily temperatures in such far-flung outposts as Vienna, Tokyo and Caribou, Maine have piqued our interest. And his dedication to the proposition that an erroneous sports prediction is better than no prediction at all has caused no end of consternation among all sports aficionados.

He has opened the trout fishing season by throwing a line into the Farmington River and pulling out a fish purchased at a store earlier the same morning. He has also opened the season by pulling a mermaid out of a hotel swimming pool.

He has regaled us with the stories of "The Lion and Albert" and "Mill Famey" more times than we can count, yet we chuckle every time he tells them. He has told us of his somewhat-less-than-successful careers as a boxer and a motorcycle rider, and we giggle no matter how many times we have heard the tales.

However, there is much more to Bob Steele than his mirth. For those in need, he devotes his bubbling good humor and warmth of spirit to a wide range of civic and charitable and community activities. His commitment to helping others is an inspiration for all of us.

Bob has become as much a part of our lives as the morning sunrise over the northeastern hills, the calm of an evening tide in a shoreline harbor, and the exuberance of a fife and drum muster in one of our centuries-old communities. His Uncle Stainless and Aunt Bessemer are relatives to each one of us.

He is living proof of the old adage that, "It isn't how long you stick around but what you put over while you are here."

As long as he sticks around, he will continue to put something over on us every morning we tune him in. And our hearts will be happier for it. This collection will rekindle many memories, yet the next time we hear one of these stories, for the umpteenth time, we will chuckle once again.

Ella Grasso

ELLA GRASSO
Governor

DEDICATION

Dedicated with deep affection to my wife, Shirley, and our sons Robert, Paul, Philip and Steven, and my dear friends:

Rhoda Life
Bertha D. Blues
John W. Sliderule
Alexander Pinkerton Slouch
Miles Apart
Farnsworth Snood
Chester Gigolo
A. Livingston Doll
Saul Wright
Helen Highwater
Cliff Dweller
Luke Outt
Sam Difference
Robin Banks
Sal Soda
Juan Meatball
L. Quentin Yerp
Hadley Brokenhearted from the Law Firm of
    Sadd & Brokenhearted
Speedy Klimmerdinger
U. Farnsworth Glick
Merging Traffic
Betty Getty
Sue LaRue
Sidney Australia (from Poquonock)
Standish Roomonly
Al Foop
Gidley Shooshfesser
Llewellyn Q. Kroke
Quinby Barnbunk

Ester Nester of Westchester
Charlie Fox of Windsor Locks
Sibelius T. Cootch
Y. U. Zunk
Fennis Birch
Hugh Miliate
Fremont McSchnook
Arno Clabyak
Justin Freep
J. Shadrack
Sol Headcheese
Oozbek Yooey
Hughey Yooey
Y. Y. Skeeber
Fats Munchausen
E. V. Fundoonis
Fred Slob
Seldom Wright
Lew Wow, the Hawaiian disc jockey
Roger Hubcap
Hillary Hardtop
Choochoo Rubingittel

Without whose tireless devotion and cooperation the preparation of this voluminous work would have been a lot easier.

BIOGRAPHY

One April first, not too many years ago, Bob Steele announced on his morning show that he had decided to accept an offer from a radio station in Chicago and he would be leaving Hartford for the Windy City. While this was just another bit of April Fool's Day tomfoolery, WTIC operators were deluged with calls imploring the station not to let Bob go and letters continued to arrive for days afterward.

Robert Lee Steele has inspired just such fanatic audience loyalty for forty-four years with an easy going blend of music, conversation, corny jokes and weather reports that has the highest "share of audience" rating of any radio program in the United States.

Bob Steele is now a Connecticut institution but he was born a long way from the Nutmeg State in Kansas City, Missouri on July 13, 1911. His parents, Hampton and Susan Steele, were divorced when Bob was five years old. Susan Steele ran a boarding house to support herself and her son, but money was hard to come by. At eight years of age, Bob got his first job delivering prescriptions for a neighborhood pharmacy. Although his salary was only $5.00 a week, by the age of twelve Bob had saved enough money to buy a motorcycle. This enabled him to take on another delivery job which paid the magnificent sum of $20.00 a week. Motorcycle racing was a natural extension of his job and Bob took to it like the proverbial duck.

Four years later, he added another enthusiasm, boxing. As Bob tells it, he was competing with a much older fellow for the attention of a girl he liked. "I thought I might have to fight her boyfriend sometime and I'd better be prepared." For $5.00, Bob took three boxing lessons and decided to enter the ring. He fought fifty-two amateur fights and won thirty, knocking out twelve opponents. This record encouraged him to turn professional—a big mistake. He fought eighteen bouts, winning only two of them and at the age of nineteen decided to retire from boxing and enter the restaurant business.

"Have you had your iron today? If not, try a Steele Sandwich" read the sign in the window of his small sandwich shop. Bob and his mother lived above the restaurant and while his mother baked cakes and pies for dessert, Bob ran the place. A year of running around on somewhat flat feet convinced Bob to sell the restaurant.

Like so many others in those Depression years, Bob was drawn to California. Even though things were tough there too, he soon found a job as a motorcycle messenger for a Los Angeles bank.

Then disaster struck! Bob decided to purchase a truck with the $750.00 proceeds from the sale of his restaurant and an additional $200.00 that he had saved. He had dreams of earning a fortune hauling produce from the farms to the city. Unfortunately, the man who sold the truck was a crook and Bob lost both the truck and all his money. "When you have no money, you worry every minute. It was a very bad time," Bob recalls.

Finally, he got a W.P.A. job as a timekeeper for $96.00 a month. He worked on a farm keeping track of the hours of all the other workers.

One day, as Bob stood in a field of carrots, a telegram arrived from a friend, George Lannom, offering him a job announcing motorcycle races in Hartford's Bulkeley Stadium. "It didn't take any time at all to make up my mind," Bob laughs. He worked all that spring and summer announcing both motorcycle races and the Savitt Gems' semi-pro baseball games. However, with the arrival of fall and the end of the racing season Bob was out of a job again.

Bob decided to go back to California. On the day before he was to leave, he went to a movie in downtown Hartford. "It was a mystery," Bob remembers, "and I arrived in the middle of it. I decided to wait until the next show began so I wouldn't spoil the plot. I had about three quarters of an hour to kill, so I wandered about a bit and finally walked into WTIC and asked for a job." Lady Luck was with Bob that day. The station needed an announcer and was in the midst of auditioning several candidates. Bob auditioned, got the job, and started work the very next day, October 1, 1936.

Bob liked working at WTIC from the start. "Everyone was friendly and people on the staff, like Leonard Patricelli, Paul Lucas, 'Bunny' Mullins, Phil Becker, George Bowe and Joe Ripley were a great help to me." At first, Bob did station breaks, commercials and introductions to the many local programs found on radio during those years. Then in 1938, he began "Strictly Sports" and his background in boxing and racing made him a natural for the show. His big chance came in 1943 when Ben Hawthorne, host of the G. Fox Morning Watch, went into the service. Bob took over the show, expanded it over the years from its original one hour length, and the morning has never belonged to anyone else.

Bob hasn't changed the content or the style of his show very much in a long time. His listeners wouldn't stand for it. Somehow they always look forward to keeping track of Bob's successes and failures in predicting the winners of sports events. Coaches have been known to call Bob and beg him not to pick their team but this doesn't seem to discourage his audience. Many folks wouldn't dream of starting the day without their "Word for the Day." Every slightly overweight Connecticut resident seems to secretly rejoice when Bob's weekly weight goes over that crucial 200 mark and they have company in their misery. Bob has become "family" to generations of New Englanders. Bob feels that way about his listeners too. Since that day in 1936, he has been late only once, by four minutes, and many times he's managed to do the show even when he was quite ill.

Despite lucrative offers from radio stations all over the country, Bob has never really considered leaving WTIC. "I couldn't leave Connecticut," Bob explains. "This is where Shirley and I have raised our four sons. This is home. The people of Connecticut have just been too good to me." In forty-four years of broadcasting, Bob Steele has been pretty good to the people of Connecticut, too.

BOB'S NEW CROP FOR '81

The Friar

A friar opened a florist shop, even though he knew this was something friars were not supposed to do. No one could persuade him to get out of the business. Finally, a long time friend of the friar's family, a man named Hugh, talked him into closing the shop and that was the origin of the slogan we hear so often today: "Only Hugh can prevent florist friars!"

The Bad Potato

A gourmet, dining in an expensive restaurant, found a dark spot in his baked potato and called his waiter.

Obviously upset, he said, "This is a BAD POTATO!"

The waiter looked down at the defective spud, slapped it smartly with his hand and said, "Shame on you!" and then to the diner, "If it gives you any more trouble, just call me!"

In the Country

A couple of fellows were out in the country and their car broke down. Unable to get it going, it was too late for any help. As darkness fell, they decided to find a place to spend the night and finally found a farm house that looked inviting. They knocked at the door and an attractive woman in her thirties answered. They told her of their problem and asked if they might spend the night. She told them she had only recently lost her husband and that she didn't think it quite proper to have them as guests. She said, however, they might stay in a barn across the road since it was her property and there was good hay in the loft. They gladly accepted and were soon bedded down. One of them awoke later and noticed the other was missing. About nine months later, the chap who had stayed in the barn got a letter from the woman's lawyer. After reading it he phoned his friend: "Fred, do you remember the night we got stuck with the car?" Fred did. "I awoke and found you gone. Did you go to the house?" Fred said he did. "Did you use my name?" Fred said he was sorry, but he did. "Well, I have a letter from the woman's lawyer and he tells me she passed away last month and left me the farm!"

RLS

AUNT BESSEMER

Mene Mene

Old Aunt Bessemer is so good to her grandchildren—she has 12 of the little moppets and they love to print their names in the dust. One thing *does* make her mad, though. When they write the date after the name.

Beauty Contest

Bonnie Sue Glubwik won $500 and a one way trip to Des Moines.

My Aunt Beth was 2nd. She won a face lift—at the Pony Tail Beauty Salon in Podunk.

Aunt Bessemer—who never was much to look at—was fined $50.

Advice from Aunt Bessemer

Drive carefully, Ladies. Remember—if you have an accident, the newspapers will list your age.

UNCLE CARBON

Safety Catch

Uncle Carbon would have lived longer if he could have gotten the safety cap off his cough medicine.

Parcel Post

My Uncle Carbon was a Pall Bearer in the Dead Letter office.

Good Old Days

Uncle Carbon is the kind of man who raves about the "good old days" while riding in an air-conditioned car in 90 degree weather.

RLS

UNCLE COLD ROLLED

Hard Sell

Uncle Cold Rolled—He's the one who said I'd rather brush with regular toothpaste and have 21% fewer commercials.

Watch It

Uncle Cold Rolled says, "A man never knows how careful he can be until he gets a new automobile, or a new pair of shoes."

Small Talk

Uncle Cold Rolled has an economy answering service. They'll answer the phone but they won't take any messages.

UNCLE CORRUGATED

Fast

Since taking up speed reading, Uncle Corrugated claims he can finish his alphabet soup in half the time.

Not Me

Uncle Corrugated said the town where he lives is terrible. Just the other morning at 3 a.m. someone was pounding and screaming at his door. But he ignored them and went on quietly playing his bagpipe.

R.I.P.

There've been many daredevils in my family. There was Uncle Corrugated who tried to thaw out a box of dynamite in the oven. He would have been 60 today.

UNCLE CRUCIBLE

Can You Spare a Dime?

Uncle Crucible went through the depression. "I remember as a kid my dad talked to me about an allowance. He said anything I could give him would be O.K."

Compliment

Compliment from Uncle Crucible: Consider yourself Steele belted!

Watch Your Step

A moment of silence, please. Today's the 50th anniversary of the passing of my Uncle Crucible. The first man to tap dance on the wing of a plane. Also the first man to be scraped off the Longmeadow town hall.

UNCLE CASE HARDENED

Collegiate

Cheerleaders at Bended Knee College in Greystone, Wyoming have the catchiest yell, I dare say, in the entire country. It's a chant that repeats and repeats the morale building words ... ON, BENDED KNEE!

Uncle Case Hardened is in his 4th year at Bended Knee and he says if he does better this year they'll make him a sophomore.

At a Loss for Words

Uncle Case Hardened Steele bought a book on dieting. Said it was delicious.

Hard as Nails

Uncle Case Hardened Steele is really tough. He once rode through Lion Country on a bicycle.

UNCLE HEAVY GAUGE

Seasonably Cool

Uncle Heavy Gauge lives in Australia where it is now autumn. He says you can always tell when it's autumn in Australia. The leaves start falling from his dining room table.

Cure All

Uncle Heavy Gauge saw an ad. "If you are deaf tear out this ad." He tore it out but he says he still can't hear.

Testimonial

Uncle Heavy Gauge was very disappointed. "It shows you what they think of you around here when you retire and they give you a testimonial during a coffee break."

UNCLE IMPORTED

Curb Service

My Uncle Imported is chauffeur for Mr. and Mrs. Walker Good. He delivers the Goods.

Enough is Too Much

My Uncle Imported said he doesn't mind suffering. It's the pain that gets him.

Repair Man

Uncle Imported loves to fix things around the house but his wife objects. His specialties—Martinis and Manhattans.

UNCLE MOLYBDENUM

On Tap

Uncle Molybdenum, my farmer uncle, is feeding his cows cocoa—so they'll give hot chocolate.

Genetics

My Uncle Molybdenum, the horticulturist, crossed a four leaf clover with poison ivy ... hoping for a rash of good luck.

Flighty

On Saturdays, Uncle Molybdenum goes to the park, tapes popcorn to the grass and watches the pigeons go crazy.

UNCLE MOLTEN

Ups and Downs

I have twin uncles, Milton and Molten. Molten's the more famous. He's in Hartford Hospital and told me,

"I'm tired today. They threw a party downstairs last night."

"So what?"

"I was the party they threw downstairs."

Get It?

Uncle Molten is the fellow who was boasting to his friends that he ran a clinic and his friends thought this was great! "What kind of clinic?", they asked. Dry Clinic and Pressing.

Hard Bitten

My Uncle Molten Steele just found out how to get 65 shaves from one blade. WINCE!

GRANDPA RUSTY

Tennis

Grandpa Rusty won a tennis match at 96 ... but it took eight people to throw him over the net.

Keep It Up

Grandpa Rusty Steele was celebrating his 100th birthday, and the reporter was interviewing him. "To what do you attribute your longevity?" the reporter asked.

Gramps thought a moment and then said, "I never smoked, drank whiskey, or stayed out late. And I always walked two miles a day."

"But," said the reporter, "I had an uncle who lived that way, yet he only lived to be 80. How do you account for that?"

Grandpa Rusty said, "He just didn't keep it up long enough."

Genealogy

Grandpa Rusty says the family tree is worth bragging about if it has consistently produced good timber, and not just nuts.

RLS

UNCLE STAINLESS

Nest Egg

Uncle Stainless looks ahead. Bought himself a couple of spare mattresses. Wants to have something to fall back on.

Sickening

As my Uncle Stainless used to say, "It's enough to make Wyatt Earp."

Alone at Last

Uncle Stainless went to a seance last night and tried to contact himself.

Durable

They say nothing is as cheap as it used to be. Obviously, they've never met my Uncle Stainless.

UNCLE TEMPERED

Instrumental

Uncle Tempered from Colebrook ... he's my night club-bing uncle ... goes to nightclubs all the time ... all the nightclubs. He takes 'em all in. Even the ones without air-conditioning. That's one thing he never worries about, he says ... the air-conditioning. He always sits in front of the tuba player.

Dead End

My Uncle Tempered's havin' a tough time. He lost his memory recently. He got a brain conclusion.

Dropkick

My uncle, Tempered Steele, "Shorty" we call him be-cause he's short tempered, is the inventor of the safety net for bar stools.

UNCLE TUBULAR

Topsy

Tubular Steele—he's my businessman uncle. He's a big wheel—running on the rim right now. He's a real non-conformist. Instead of bringing his lunch in an attache case as many of us do ... he carries his business papers in his lunch pail.

High Pressure

Uncle Tubular just came back from a weekend in Vermont and griped about his motel. Said the towels were so thick he could hardly get his suitcase closed.

Greaser

Uncle Tubular makes a skin lotion for pigs. OINKment.

UNCLE WELDED

The Road Not Taken

As Uncle Welded always says, "Show me a job with a challenge and I will call in sick."

Assembly Line

Uncle Welded gets up each morning ... puts on his hair piece ... his glasses ... his dentures. Aunt Bess calls it getting his head together.

Hot and Cold

Uncle Welded's brother-in-law has rubber pockets so he can steal soup.

OPENING THE PROGRAM

**(While reading this page, please hum,
"A Hunt in the Black Forest.")**

Early

Opening at 5:30 a.m. "Well, how do you like the show so far?"

Honesty

As you may notice, the jokes on my program are usually adult stories—they are 21 years of age or older.

Eyes Ahead

All right—sit right down and stare at your radio. I'll be looking back at you for 4½ hours.

Live

The program you're about to hear is
 LIVE—
Maybe not lively
 but LIVE—
My name is BOB FRIDAY—and it's Bob every other day—Bob Steele.
And our music man is BOB TOO. Mr. and Mrs. Too's
 boy, Bob.

BOB IN 3-D: DIET, DINING and DOCTORS

Santa

I've got troubles. I tried on my Santa suit last night and it's a perfect fit. That's not the trouble ... I just discovered I don't need the pillow tied to my waist this year.

Tailor

Tailor, when measuring a waistline: "It's amazing when you realize that a Douglas Fir with that girth would be ninety feet tall!"

(My weight today: 197 lbs. 4⅔ oz.)

Loss

Bryant Thomas told me that over the past three months he lost 13 pounds. I think I found them!

Filling Station

A listener in Columbia says she figured it was time to go on a diet when the guy at the Filling Station asked her if she wanted her shoes rotated after 4,000 miles.

Religiously

I don't know why she's so fat. She says she diets religiously.

THAT JUST MEANS SHE DOESN'T EAT IN CHURCH.

London

I told her I had just come back from London where I had lost 20 pounds in two weeks. She wanted to know how much that was in American money.

Fat Cat

He who indulges ... bulges.

Dieticians

Dieticians tell you to starve yourself to death if you want to live longer.

Poor

Many of us don't know what poor losers we are until we try dieting.

Worrying

Worrying makes you lose weight—unless it's your weight you're worrying about.

Snack

For me, an afternoon snack is a pause that re-fleshes.

Cars

Harry in Hamden writes that by the time a man can afford to buy one of those little sports cars, he's too fat to get into one.

Pill

New reducing pill that will allow you to take off 10 lbs. in one week. Take one before each meal. When you wake up, the food is gone.

Vintage

A listener in New Haven wants to know the proper wine to serve with Hamburger Helper.

English

I could tell he was English. He was eating alphabet soup and he kept dropping his H's.

Sale

The meat market is having a white sale ... all fat.

Dairy

A Greenwich grocer ran an ad once that read: "You can whip our cream but you can't beat our milk."

Tip

I've been reading a health book that says garlic is fatal to mosquitoes. That may be true, but the hard part is getting them to eat the veal and peppers.

Bologna

Two flies found some bologna clinging to the handle of a butcher knife. After eating all they could hold, they took off, only to fall to the ground with a thud. The moral of the story is ... don't fly off the handle when you're full of bologna!

Flavoring

Little girls are no longer made of sugar and spice and everything nice. They're made of sucaryl, artificial flavoring and polyunsaturated fats.

Turkey

I've decided we're not going to have the usual Thanksgiving turkey this year. This year we're gonna get a new one.

Substitute

A listener from Torrington sent me a postcard: "Think of how much easier it would be on the wives around Thanksgiving if the Pilgrims had shot a peanut butter sandwich instead."

Household Tip

Keeping ice cubes in warm water makes them difficult to find again.

Crocked Pot

Recipe for Elephant Stew

1 Elephant (medium size)   2 Rabbits (Optional)

Salt and Pepper

Cut the elephant into small bite-size pieces. This should take about two months. Add enough brown gravy to cover. Cook over a kerosene fire for about four weeks at 465 degrees.

This will serve thirty-eight hundred people. If more are expected, two rabbits may be added. (Do this only if necessary as most people do not like to find hare in their stew.)

First Step

Burglar's Omelet—Pencils ready? All right: First, steal two fresh eggs ...

Homestyle

This morning I had breakfast at a restaurant that features home-style breakfasts. The waitress wears a bathrobe and gym shoes.

Blackout

Two hillbillies who had never been on a train were drafted and on their way to camp. A man came through the train selling bananas, which neither mountaineer had ever seen before. Each of them bought one. As one of them bit into his banana the train entered a tunnel. His voice came to his companion through the darkness:

"Have you et yours yet?"

"Not yet. Why?"

"Well, don't touch it. I've et one bite and gone blind."

Gift

"You're giving me a lot of bone there, aren't you?" asked the lady.

"I'm not giving it to you," said the butcher. "You're paying for it."

Carp

A listener offers a great recipe for cooking carp: Clean and skin your fish, then fasten to a well-scrubbed board. Season, place in oven until done. Remove. Place carp in garbage can and eat the board.

Coconut

And then there's the listener in Talcottville who writes that his wife gave him a cake with coconut topping. I told her she knew I hated coconut. She said, "Eat it. It's only lint."

Bagel

A Martian stepped from his flying saucer and entered a delicatessen. Pointing to a bagel he said, "Give me that wheel."

"That's not a wheel," the proprietor said, "That's a bagel. You eat it. Here, try it."

The Martian took a bite. His face lit up. "Hey," he said, "this could go swell with lox!"

Choice

Customer: "Say, what kind of pie is this, apple or peach?"
   Waitress: "What does it taste like?"
   Customer, tasting, "Glue!"
   Waitress: "Then it's peach. The apple tastes like putty."

Limit

A man saw a sign in a window of a restaurant that said, "All you can eat for $3.95." He entered, helped himself at the buffet and when he went back for a second helping, they turned him down. "That's all you can eat for $3.95," they told him.

Fish Story

Pat's conscience was battling with his appetite one Friday when he saw the man at the next table dig into a thick, juicy steak. "Give me a whale sandwich on rye bread with French fries," he told the waitress.

"Whale? That's not on the menu, sir," she replied.

"Then bring me a thick sirloin. The Lord knows I asked for fish."

Bill

"Waiter, I find that I have just enough money to pay for the dinner, but I have nothing in the way of a tip for you."

"Let me add up that bill again, sir."

Dutch Treat

In a German restaurant the waiter said "Coffee?"
   I said "nein."
   He brought me 9 cups of coffee!

Fussy

Fussy diner in a Rocky Hill restaurant, "Yes, waiter, I'll have lamb chops, mashed potatoes, peas and salad. And make the chops lean."

Waiter, "Which way, sir?"

Heavy

In my favorite Chinese restaurant (where they chop their own suey), I asked for soup. Waiter said, "What kind?"

I said, "Wonton."

He brought me two thousand pounds of soup.

Helpful

And then there's the story of the Wallingford waitress asking her customer if he wanted pie with his dinner. "Is it customary?" asked the diner.

"No," said the waitress, "it's blueberry."

Poem

A gentleman dining in Kew
Found a very large gnat in his stew
Said the waiter, "Don't shout
Or wave it about
Or the rest will be wanting one too."

Sport

This happened in a restaurant on Route 44. "What's this fly doing in my soup?" inquired the angry diner. The waiter stood a minute looking into the soup bowl, "Looks like the backstroke to me."

Ears

Told my doc ... "I got a ringing in my ear."

He said, "Don't answer it."

Psychiatrist

Message on a postcard received by a psychiatrist from a vacationing patient from Pomfret: "Having a wonderful time. Why?"

Hospital

A listener from Goshen dropped me a note complaining: "Like when you're in the hospital. People come to see you but they throw their coat on top of you and talk to the guy in the next bed."

Dentist

My dentist has a special. In by 9:00, out by noon with a whole new set of teeth and your car washed.

Man Made

Did you read about that scientist who created the first man made virus? You know what that means. This year, for the first time in history, there's gonna be enough flu to go around.

Lawn Mower

A wife went to a New Haven psychiatrist for advice about her husband who was imagining himself to be a lawn mower.

"Pure fantasy," the doctor said. "It will pass away."

"It had better pass away," the wife said. "I'm getting tired of lending him to the neighbors."

Doubling

My doctor has decided to double his practice ... he cut down on his office hours and uses the time on the golf course.

Explosion

PJR writes from Montville to report that there was a loud explosion in the back room of a drug store.

The pharmacist staggered out, his face stained with smoke, his glasses broken and his jacket in shreds.

He said to the lady customer, "Have your doctor write out that prescription again—and this time tell him to print it."

Hypochondriacs

There's a Guilford couple I know. They're both a little eccentric and both hypochondriacs. For her birthday last week he gave her a $5,000 gift certificate to the Mayo Clinic.

Question

A question from a listener in Monson, Massachusetts: "What is an antidote?"

A medicine that we take to prevent dotes.

Transplants

The newest thing is transplanting organs from animals to humans. I know a guy who got a cocker spaniel's heart. He feels as good as new, but now he's bothered by fleas.

Fight

Fight America's #1 killer ... Natural Causes.

Medical?

First little boy in a Rockville General Hospital ward: "Are you medical or surgical?"

Second little boy: "I don't know. What does that mean?"

First little boy: "Were you sick when you came here, or did they make you sick after you got here?"

Flu

It's easy to tell when you have the flu. You ache all over and feel numb—sort of like Orson Welles sat on you.

X-Rays

The Doc was looking at my x-rays. He said, "You know, there's not a mean bone in your body."

Theatre

I just heard about a movie about a psychiatrist. The theatre is taking out all the seats and putting in couches.

Check

An Enfield listener tells me about his cousin's experience.

Doctor: "I don't like to mention it, but that check you gave me came back."

Patient: "What a coincidence, Doc, so did my rheumatism."

Virus

"Virus" is a term used by doctors meaning ... "Your guess is as good as mine."

Shingle

Then there's the tale of the young doctor who hung up his shingle in a small town and waited for his first patient. Some days later one arrived ... covered from head to foot with an angry, dangerous looking rash. The puzzled young medico hastily consulted his textbooks but could find no help there. Finally he said to the patient, "Did you ever have this affliction before?"

"Oh, sure, Doc," the patient replied. "I've had it twice before."

"Well, damnation," diagnosed the doctor, "you've got it again."

Bicycle

A Norwich doctor writes to say that the bicycle rider is unlikely to die of a heart attack. The chances, naturally, are that he will be run over first.

Dime

A man had trouble hearing 'til he went to the neighborhood doctor, who promptly extracted a dime from the guy's ear.

"You're marvelous!" cried the patient. "I can hear perfectly now. It was there for three months!"

"You mean you knew it? Why didn't you take it out?" asked the baffled medico.

The man shrugged his shoulders. "I didn't need the money then."

Fading

I remember a few years ago when I called my doctor at 3 a.m. and gasped: "I'm fading fast!"

He said, "Get a sun lamp!"

Sinus

Do you have a sinus problem?
Do you sneeze a lot?
Do you cough continuously?
Do what thousands do! Go to the movies.

Operation

When the doctor told his patient he needed an operation, the patient wanted to know what it would cost.

Said the doctor, "Two hundred dollars."

"Would it be dangerous?" asked the patient.

"Don't be silly," scoffed the doctor. "For $200 you couldn't buy a dangerous operation."

Germ

Mama germ to papa germ, at the height of the flu season: "If you can't call, virus."

Benefit

A doctor and a young man met at a cocktail party.

"I want to thank you, doctor," said the young man, "for the benefit I have gained from your treatment."

The doctor looked at him blankly. "But I don't think you are a patient of mine," he finally said.

"No, I'm not," came the cheerful reply. "But my uncle was, and I'm his heir."

Aspirin

Talk about your studies: Nine out of ten doctors recommend aspirin. One prefers headaches.

Gone

Cohen drops dead at his office, and his secretary calls Mrs. Cohen: "Terrible news. Your husband is dead."

Mrs. C. says, "Give him some chicken soup right away!"

Secretary replies, "But he's dead, Mrs. Cohen. The soup can't help him."

Mrs. C. insists, "It can't do him any harm!"

Don't Answer

Patient: "Doc, what can I do about this constant ringing in my ear?"

Doc: "Get an unlisted ear."

Language

A Waterford listener tells me that when he was an intern at Kings County Hospital in Brooklyn, a common complaint of the natives was "bronicle trouble." Soon this local pronunciation sounded quite correct to him. So he understood perfectly when an elderly asthmatic patient said, "Doc, I'm worried. I got a chronicle bronicle condition."

Help

"Doc, every time I bend over and put my hands below my knees and bring them up above my waist, I get a terrible pain."

"Well, why would you make those silly motions?"

"How else can I get my pants on?"

Extension

Frank Amfler, a friend of mine in Kansas City, told me his doctor gave him six months to live—but Frank said when he couldn't pay his bill the doctor gave him another six months.

Sad

I just heard a sad story. It's about a doctor who lost all his money because the stock market went down. To save himself he tried in desperation to rob a bank ... but nobody could read his hold-up note.

Cheerful

Cheerful people, the doctors say, resist disease better than the glum ones. In other words, it's the surly bird who catches the germ.

Baby

Excited man on telephone: "Nurse, tell the doctor to come quick. My wife is having a baby."

Nurse: "He'll be right there, but meanwhile follow these instructions. I suppose this is her first baby?"

Man: "No, this is her husband."

Quotations

A Westport listener tells me she's eagerly awaiting the announced book of *Familiar Medical Quotations*. She wants to know what wise physician first said, "You have to expect these things at your age," "There's a lot of it going around," and "Hmmmm!"

Shaking

The doctor noticed that the hands of a patient kept shaking during the physical examination. "You drink a lot, don't you?" the doctor asked.

"No, sir," the patient replied, "I spill most of it."

THE SPORTING SIDE OF STEELE

The Extra Point

The ultimate application of the platoon system has recently been suggested by a group of Connecticut football coaches.

They want a platoon for offense, one for defense, and one to go to classes.

Limit

Uncle Stainless' hobby is fly-fishing for sardines. The daily limit is 10,000.

Coaching

One day at the Dodgers' training camp at Vero Beach, Coach Charlie Dressen talked to one of his young infielders in the locker room.

"Remember all those batting tips, double-play pivots, and base-running hints I gave you this afternoon?" he asked.

"I sure do, coach," the boy replied.

"Well, forget 'em," Charlie said. "We just traded you to the Braves."

Drought

The drought in California has even gotten to baseball. When they yank a pitcher, they no longer send him to the showers, they send him to the drycleaners.

A Subtle Warning

A Nutmeg basketball coach was congratulated one night by the college president. The coach asked, "Would you like me as much if we didn't win?"

"I'd like you just as much," the president replied, "but I'd miss having you around."

Football Slush

I'm told that one of the most unpleasant football games ever played occurred some years ago on a Thanksgiving Day in Philadelphia. In the midst of a deluge of snow and rain, the Cornell captain won the toss and bitterly stared out over Franklin Field, covered with cold, gray slush.

"Do we have to play football in that fluid?" he demanded.

"Yes," was the implacable reply. "Which end do you want?"

"Well," said the player, "We'll kick with the tide."

Karate Chop

Have you heard about the Karate expert who rolled down the window of his car to signal for a left hand turn? He chopped a Volkswagen in half!

Ladies' Day

Two elderly ladies arrived at a Farmington baseball game just as the batter hit a home run. They sat watching the game in silence until—several innings later—the same batter came up to bat and hit another home run.

Said one of the ladies to the other: "Let's go. This is where we came in."

Scoreboard

I know a local sports announcer who thinks Hawaii Five-0 is a final score!

Unfair

Two fisherman sitting on a Mystic bridge, their lines in the water below, made a bet as to who would catch the first fish. One got a bite and got so excited that he fell off the bridge.

"Oh, well," said the other, "if you're going to dive for them, the bet's off."

Close One

That football player who, a couple of years ago, was charged with shaving points—I was wondering if the fact that he was endorsing a certain razor blade on TV was of any importance. Suppose there was a connection there?

Indian Hill Curse

On your first day on the course—may you get a hole in one without a single witness.

Pardon Me

The standard excuse is that the hunter, shot by a companion, was mistaken for some species of wild animal. And the wild animal which is run over by a motorcar was, we suppose, mistaken for a pedestrian.

Nags

Lady jockeys may be OK but would you want your brother to marry one?

Good, Berra, Best

Yogi said—If people don't wanta come out to the ball park—you can't keep 'em away.

Hole in One

We were playing on a field adjacent to a farm. I fouled a pitch and when the ball sailed into the cistern the manager said, "Steele, that was a well hit ball." (Nicest compliment he ever paid me!)

Hunting

After long arguments, an Ellington sportsman finally agreed to take his wife on a hunting trip to Africa. When they returned months later, he had virtually no trophies, but his wife proudly displayed a superb lion's head.

"Did she hit it with that Magnum rifle you bought her?" a friend asked the husband.

"No," he replied sourly, "she hit it with the 1961 station wagon we rented."

New Referee

A Rocky Hill listener's brother became a basketball referee ... because when he got out of jail he didn't want to waste the shirt.

Fisherman's Luck

Lugging a huge fish, a Granby angler met another fishing enthusiast whose catch consisted of twelve small ones. "Howdy," said the Granby man as he gingerly laid down his fish and waited for comment. The other fellow stared for a few moments and calmly responded,

"Just caught the one, eh?"

Horses

I bet on one horse that really had good breeding. When he came out of the starting gate he turned around to close it behind him.

Bull fights

Bull fighting is the most popular sport in Latin America. You may think it's revolting, but revolting is actually the second most popular sport.

Retirement

Jack Sharkey, the old former world heavyweight champion, lived in placid retirement in Epping, NH, a hamlet of 2,023 people. He had most of his ring earnings, all his faculties and his wife, Dorothy, whom he courted and married in Epping 49 years before. "I'm in good shape," he said. "I've got everything I need here. The doctor lives right there across the street, the druggist is on the corner, you can see the funeral parlor from here and the cemetery is right up the street."

Pig Skin

They played with a real pig skin in 1880. Used a real pig. If you fumbled, the game was sometimes delayed for hours.

Then in 1890 they changed to a chicken. Made it easier on kick offs too.

Fast Ride

Watching water-skiing for the first time, the Indian asked, "Why boats go so fast?"

And the second Indian said, "Man on string chase 'im."

Short Fights

The fight manager was grousing. "My boy is no good in short fights," he said. "He needs 10 rounds." But preliminary fighters just don't get 10 round fights, so he finally had to settle for a six-rounder.

After ten seconds in the first round at the Hartford Coliseum the fighter was flat on the canvas, out like a light.

"You see!" howled his manager. "I told you he's no good in short fights!"

Spring

Spring! When fishermen get that far away lake in their eyes.

Navigation

An Essex yachtsman, who had just been initiated into the mysteries of the art of navigation, suddenly put aside his sextant and shouted to his companion, "Take off your hat."

"Why should I?" asked his bewildered friend.

"Because according to my calculations," replied the Yachtsman, "we are in the center of St. Patrick's Cathedral."

Mountain Climbing

I was mountain climbing. The guide said, "Don't slip. It's an 8,000 ft. drop. But if you do, look to the left. It's a terrific view!"

Record

My Uncle Cold Rolled, the famous Savitt Gems ball player, once set a record for the most four letter words used against a left handed pitcher in a single game.

Another Record

My uncle also set a record for the most flies caught. In his hotel room.

Pachaug Pond

Fisherman's Lament: A 3-pound pull, a 5-pound bite, an 8-pound jump, and a 10-pound fight, a 12-pound bend to your pole—but alas! When you get him aboard he's a half-pound bass.

Sky High

Wilt Chamberlain is so tall he has to stand on a box to brush his teeth!

Kangaroo Hunt

Visiting Australia, a Haddam man decided to go on a kangaroo hunt. He rented a jeep and told the driver to look for a kangaroo. They reached the wide-open spaces and they spotted one. The driver pursued. They went at breakneck speed without gaining on the animal. Finally, the Haddam man shouted, "There's no use chasing that thing."

"Why not?" asked the driver.

"'Cause we're doing' 65, and that critter ain't even put his front feet down yet!"

Football Future

University of Connecticut educators predict the day is at hand for teaching without books. Then you will really see some football teams.

Injuries

In school he was a great athlete. He was only hurt twice. Once in the huddle ... and once when the bench fell over.

Bookmaker Odds

The bookmaker was very disturbed when his young daughter came in at 20 to 1.

Halftime

I'll never forget the time. It was halftime at the Syracuse-Colgate football game, as the college band left the field, Syracuse marched proudly to the center of the stadium and quickly spelled out the word ... Pepsodent.

Racing

"Are you planning to race your horse?"
  "You bet I am, and I think I can beat him."

Deep Freeze!

It was in the wintertime. I think I was with Bill Lee. We went into the hotel and it was colder inside than outside. When we went into the room our breath was coming out like smoke. Our teeth were chattering. Bill looked at me and said how come the light didn't go out when we shut the door?

Baseball Law

Some things you just can't do. For instance, in baseball, there's no way a pitcher can scatter 37 hits.

Good Advice

About being a fighter: My trainer said—make him come to you—and when he does—stay away from him!

Fair Decision

Home town decisions were so tough I had to knock him out to get a draw!

Togetherness

Ever wonder why mountain climbers are always roped together? It's to keep the sensible ones from going home.

Bowling Alley

I wanted to bowl last night—but there was a strike down at our neighborhood bowling alleys.

Baseball Statistics

If the distance between a fan and the end of the row is more than nine seats, he will order a hot dog.

A baseball, if hit into the stands, will stay there.

If a baseball argument is continued indefinitely, that's only natural.

The wrangles of any two players are together less than one umpire.

An umpire is equal to a sum of pop bottles.

Long Red

Now the Russians show up with a 7-foot, 3-inch basketball player. Who leaked them the blueprints?

License?

Answer to a Port Jefferson listener: No, you do not need a hunting license to shoot pool in this state.

Hot Dog!

Here's Billy Frankfurter—Wiener and still champ!

James Bond

I was the James Bond of baseball. My batting average was .007.

Fore

Going golfing? If you drink, don't drive … don't even putt.

Nerve

Golf is a game that requires iron nerve. For example, looking an opponent in the eye and saying: "That was a practice swing."

Form

My golfing partner had a bad round, threw his clubs in a pond and started for the water, himself, saying, "I'm gonna drown myself."

I said. "You can't drown yourself."

He said, "Why not?"

I said, "You can't keep your head down.

Model

Two guys standing at fireplace, host is showing guest a ship model he has constructed inside a bottle. Guest: "If you think that was hard, you should try getting a golf ball into a 4½ inch cup."

Natural

A Simsbury golfer whose game had gone from awful to terrible finally decided he'd better go to a pro and take some lessons. The pro took him out to the practice tee, handed him a driver and said, "Now first let me see you take your full swing without hitting the ball."

"What!" screamed the golfer. "Why should I pay you good money to teach me something I'm doing already?"

Spiked

… I can't believe it. Forgive me if I'm in an awful mood, but I think you'll understand. Would you believe that my wife threw out my golf shoes?? … She said, the nails were coming out the bottom.

Near Miss

… I'm really a great golf fan, but I don't think I'm doing too well. The closest I ever came to a hole-in-one … was a seven!

Skill

On their exhibition tour in Japan, the St. Louis baseball Cardinals are playing on a lot of fields where there's no grass, and Stan Musial said, "It's like spending two hours in the same sand trap."

He must be a lousy golfer. The sand trap hasn't been built that I can't get out of in 35 minutes.

Mix Up

The modern-day mother encourages her little boy by saying, "Eat your spinach, dear, so you can grow up to be a big boy and hit home runs like Gary Player."

Short Cut

... Hey ... I've found a great way to take ten strokes off your golf game ... It's called an eraser.

No Fault

A West Hartford golfer was in an important Wampanaug tournament when his caddie was stricken with hiccups. The golfer, a deliberate putter, flinched at each hiccup.

On the last hole, facing a short putt that would win the tournament for him, he hesitated over his ball. Finally, he stroked it. The ball stopped short of the cup.

He turned to his caddie. "See what you made me do?" he yelled. "You and your hiccups!"

"But I didn't hiccup that time," the caddle protested.

"I know," snarled the golfer. "But I had allowed for it."

Pray

When you are playing golf, always say a prayer when you tee off. It helps you remember to keep your head down.

Brassy

A fellow who was a guest of a club member at Wethersfield Golf Club was playing a difficult water hole. He drove his ball into the pond and then turned to his host and asked him to supply another as he had no spares.

He promptly drove it into the pond again and did the same with the third and fourth balls.

"Sam," the host protested, "these are my new $1.25 golf balls you're losing."

"Listen, Jim," replied the duffer, "If you can't afford the game, you shouldn't be playing it."

Help

Golfer is in very deep trouble in rough and woods ... caddie tells him: "If I were you I'd use a 9-iron and cheat a little!"

Fun

If you watch a game, it's fun. If you play, it's religion. If you work at it, it's golf.

Statistics

I can't help but laugh when I think about golf. What's funnier than a man taking a ball 1½ inches in diameter, placing it on another ball 8,000 miles in diameter and trying to hit the little one without hitting the big one.

Cheater

"Why don't you play golf with George anymore?" Pete's wife asked him.

"Would you play with a fellow who puts down the wrong score and moves the ball when you aren't watching?"

"No," she replied.

"Neither will George."

Club Flush

Two golfers were annoyed by a slow couple in front of them, obviously new to the game. At one hole, there was a particularly long wait. One of the offenders dawdled on the fairway while his companion searched industriously in the rough.

"Why don't you help your friend find his ball?" one shouted.

"Oh, he's got his ball," he replied blandly, "he's looking for his club."

Locker Sign

In locker room of Farmington country club: "Please drive carefully—last week three members were hit by golf balls."

Choice

When the wife came upstairs to the bedroom, she found her husband in bed with his golf clubs. As she stared at him, he said: "When we had that argument over my playing golf all day, you said I had to make a choice. Well, I made it."

Juvenile

A marble tournament was in full swing. Little Johnny missed an easy shot and in a loud voice uttered a real cuss word. A preacher who was among the spectators called to him: "Johnny, what happens to little boys who swear?" Replied little Johnny, "They grow up to be golfers."

Success

The threshold of success is hiring a neighbor's kid to mow your lawn while you play golf for exercise.

PUNNING AROUND WITH RLS

BOB STEELE

Balderdash

It is no wonder that the front row seats at hit shows are usually filled by baldheaded men—you can only get those seats from scalpers.

Mystic

"What's the name of that mystic from Australia?"
"The Kang Guru."

Gossip

She's a good kid, but she can smell out the latest gossip from a mile away. She's got a fine scent of rumor.

Bad Dream

The Quinnipiac freshman had gone to sleep in English class and the professor threw a book at him. "What hit me?" he asked, startled. "That," said the professor, "was a flying Chaucer."

Why, Of Coarse

"Madam, I represent the Goat Mountain Wool Company—Would you be interested in some coarse yarns?"

"Sure, go ahead ... let's hear a couple."

Bird Fancier

Baxter H. Fungus, Music Instructor in Storrs, Connecticut (or was it at Dwindle Tech in Foonhide, Vermont) taught a mynah bird to sing and a pigeon to hum. Imagine, a humming pigeon!

Bonanza

A Woodstock customer asked a stationer's clerk to advise him on the selection of a greeting card. "I want to send a card to a man who is drilling for oil on my property," the man said, "but I've been unable to find an appropriate card. What would you suggest?"

"I think you ought to send him a 'get well' card," the clerk replied.

Cash and Curry

A backwoodsman came to the town store and asked for a can of talcum. The clerk asked, "Mennen's?"

He replied, "No, wimmen's."

The clerk asked, "You want it scented?"

"No, I'll take it with me."

Howler

How can we be sure it's a dogwood tree? By its bark.

Hard Shell

An elephant was drinking from an African river when he saw a snapping turtle sleeping on a log. He walked over to the turtle and kicked it clear to the other side.

"Why did you do that?" asked a giraffe.

"Because I recognized him as the same turtle who bit my trunk 50 years ago."

"What a fantastic memory!" exclaimed the giraffe.

"Yes," agreed the elephant modestly, "I am blessed with turtle recall."

Union Suits

The elves that work for Santa Claus are in the union now. They're in the A.F. of Elves.

Overeating

This moth and his mate had come upon a discarded pair of all wool pearl buttoned spats and proceeded to stuff themselves, finishing one but being too uncomfortable to partake of the other. Mr. Moth took a little flight to relieve the fullness and ran into an old friend who greeted him with "Hiya, Joe! Howya feelin'?" To which Joe replied, "Not so hot. Just had a spat with the wife."

The Cabinet

Every new President appoints fact-finders and trouble shooters but usually winds up with trouble finders and fact shooters.

Collision

A truck full of cotton collided with a truck loaded with chickens and it took two hours for the cotton-picking chicken pluckers and the chicken-picking cotton pluckers to clean up the mess.

Friendly

At a track meet: "Pardon me, are you a Pole Vaulter?" "No, I'm a Ukrainian. But how did you know my name was Valter?"

Money Talks

Conversation overheard in a beauty parlor in Ledyard. Hairdresser: "Shall I give you a shampoo, Madam?" Mrs. Gotrocks: "I can afford the best—you'll give me a genuine poo or nothing at all!"

Lost in Space

"I lived in Yuma for awhile once. I was a cab driver, but I was fired after a few weeks. I couldn't seem to find streets and addresses. I had a map of Yuma, but I just couldn't savvy it. I guess I just didn't have any sense of Yuma."

Russians

We know what a Czar is. Now his wife would be a Czarina, right? And their children, of course, would be Czardines!

Whistler

Whistler came home one day and found his mother scrubbing the kitchen floor on her hands and knees. "Why, Mother," he exclaimed, "have you gone off your rocker?"

Builder

Napoleon Bone is building a new hotel-apartment house in Hartford, to be known as the Napoleon Bone Apartments.

Round & Round

I was a spokesman in a bicycle repair shop.

Tune Title

What is the official "Song of the Moth?" You came to me from out of mohair.

Salty

There was a storekeeper whose name was Mr. Bye. Some children came in his store and bought potato chips. As they were leaving they said, "Good Chips, Mr. Bye."

Bow-wow

The man in court was sorrowfully relating his experience: "Then the dog chased me and I clambered up the tree where I got a huge splinter in this leg."

"Ah, yes," cut in the magistrate, "you found the bark worse than the bite, eh?"

Spring's Coming

What with the kids running across the yard, it won't be lawn now.

What Else?

ONE: "Where have you been lately, Dr. Jekyll?"
ANOTHER: "Hyding."

Poem

"Ben met Anna, made a hit.
Grew a beard, Ben-Anna split."

Doublecross

A listener from Bloomfield claims he crossed a doorbell with a bumblebee and got a humdinger.

Shakeup

News: A man was arrested in a cafe—charged with assault with intent to pepper.

Libretto

What does the bride think when she walks into the church? Aisle, altar, hymn.

Rocker

No matter what they say, I still think Whistler's Mother was framed!

Trip

What is the definition of an Apache hitchhiker?
Answer: Indian Thummer.

Takeoff

Tern of the Century: Most remarkable bird of the last 100 years.

Drip

As drops of rainwater landed in his cell, a convict yelled, "Hey, Warden! This pen leaks!"

Weather Note

Magistrate: "Driving through the red light will cost you $10 and costs, and the next time you'll go to jail, understand?"

Culprit: "Yes, your Honor, just like a weather report—fine today, cooler tomorrow."

Comrade

People felt sorry for the poor little Russian boy with his arms full of newspapers. But Ivan held his head high with pride, for after all, he did have a clutch of Tass.

Eye Opener

Then there was the farmer in Colebrook who named his rooster Robinson because he crew so.

Rock A Baby

A Lebanon listener who just sailed to Europe writes that he was sea-sick all the way over. Says he was overcome with a motion.

Retired

Marge: "My husband is always under my feet."
Shirley: "Oh! He's retired?"
Marge: "No. He's a midget!"

Vintage

He refers to his hangover as ... "The Wrath of Grapes."

No Gnus is Good Gnus

A gnu was donated to a local zoo and temporarily placed in an unfinished cage. The next morning it was discovered that the cage had been cleaned, the floor repaired. The zookeeper remarked, "We're lucky to have a typical gnu and tiler too."

All Aboard

I remember the lean days ... when I had to sleep at the bus station or the railroad station. And I wasn't alone. In those days MANY A BRAVE HEART WAS ASLEEP IN THE DEPOT.

Rock Group

4 carpenters formed a tuba group—The Tuba Four.

Ouch

Then there's the bank teller who stole money—gambled successfully and then returned the money with interest. He returned more to the safe than he took out. That was his undoing. They noticed it and he was sentenced for being generous TO A VAULT.

Sale

"Your new overcoat is pretty loud, isn't it?"
"Yes, but I intend to buy a muffler to go with it."

Weight Out

Want to know how to make a cigarette lighter?
... Take out the tobacco, silly.

Instrumental

George Gershwin, touring Cape Cod with several musical colleagues, couldn't decide whether to rehearse a rhapsody or spend the afternoon cycling along the beach. He asked: "Which shall it be—do we get down to work, or shall we bike up the strand?"

Condo

In Haiti, the staple item of food is rice, which is grown both in the fields and also (a special variety) in the hills. The Haitians who grow the mountain-type rice separate their plots of ground into areas called apartments. This, of course, gives them the distinction of owning the earliest known type of high-rice apartments.

Introduction

Mr. Wendell, the builder—Oliver Wendell. You've heard of Oliver Wendell Homes.

Crossing

The Mexican was explaining to the American that his wife had had an accident with a wheezle. Asked the American, "Did the weasel bite her?" "No," replied the Mexican. "She was crossing the track and she didn't hear the wheezle."

Schoolboy Essay

A housewife in Bridgeport threw some old prunes off the back step. Sitting on a nearby pump handle, a crow flew down, snatched a prune, flew back, ate it, flew down, flew back—and after the forty-second prune, dropped dead, proving that you should never fly off the handle when you're full of prunes.

Franges

A Groton listener tells me: There was this new guy working in the Parts Department. He couldn't find a thing. He spent 20 minutes looking for a franges cover for a 1926 Chandler. "I thought you told me you'd been around motors all your life," growled the boss. New mechanic smiled up from a tangle of nuts, bolts, coils and stuff.

"Nope," he confessed, "I'm a stranger to these parts."

Up Up

The price of Henways is going up. (What's a Henway?) Oh, 2½—3 pounds.

What's That?

And then there's the gentleman from Griswold who did his bathroom in wood paneling. He's a member of the Birch John Society.

Now Hear This

Diaper is my word for the day. Which reminds me: The safety pin is now 100 years old, but there have been a lot of changes since it was invented.

Who?

I know a fellow whose name is Will Knott. He never writes his name in full. He just signs it "Won't."

Scotch Broth

There once was a Tlingit Eskimo chief who, witnessing his first caber tossing exhibition, commented—Hmmm— him really totem pole!

Heaven

A divinity student named Fiddle would not accept his degree. He said, "It's enough to be Fiddle without being Fiddle D.D."

What?

"What do you think of cyclamates?"

"I'm for 'em. What's wrong with a guy and his wife riding bikes together?"

Think Ahead

Friend of mine, Thomas N. Terry, was thrown off a plane because of his initials on his attaché case.

All Over

Doctors hate to come to your home. Same thing in Africa, even. Witch doctors are refusing to make hut calls.

Cute

A Waterbury old-timer tells me they once had an ice man there who was going on the radio but they couldn't hear him. He got nervous when he saw the microphone and got tong-tied.

Mental Health

My brother is a motorcycle nut.
He ought to see a cycle-analyist.

Pet Rabbit

There was this guy in Derby who had a pet rabbit. It got sick one day so he took it to the veterinarian and the vet proceeded to examine it. "I can't understand, Doc," the guy said. "I give my rabbit the best of care. I even give it goat's milk to drink." The vet no sooner heard this than he handed the rabbit back to his owner.

"No wonder," he said, "you should know better than to use that greasy kid stuff on your hare."

Electronic Brain

What happens when a good-looking girl is mixed with an electronic brain?
You get a calculating blonde.

Self-Service

Why not a self-service hospital where you can suture-self?

Information

Are you the man who sells the sweet potatoes? I yam.

Notice

Wall to wall carpeting is hard to beat.

Lost and Found

Please tell me where I can get a jiffy to dry my nylon gloves in?

Wry

B.E. of Vernon writes: I call my Dachshund "Pumpernickel" because she's German bred.

Television

I've been watching that quiz program for basketball fans—Dribble or Nothing.

No, I Wouldn't

Would you say that a person wearing a wig is going around under an assumed mane?

I Wonder

Why is it that shipments go by car and cargo goes by ship?

Soap Opera

Why did the Eskimo take a bath in the tide?
Cause it was COLD OUT TIDE.

Crusty

In the Middle Ages when entertainers were scarce, many a king hired short, pint-sized jesters because they realized that half an oaf is better than none!

Marginal

The bulls and the bears aren't nearly as responsible for stock market disasters as the bum steers.

A BOB'S EYE VIEW OF BEARS, BULLS AND BUSINESS

CLICK

CLICK

CLICKETY

RLS

Help

The harrassed taxpayer was undergoing intensive grilling by an Internal Revenue Service man when he suddenly blurted out, "It's times like this that I wish the Indians had fought harder!"

Assets & Liabilities

I just saw a modern day version of FAUST. In the first act he sells his soul to the Devil. Then he spends the rest of the opera trying to convince Internal Revenue it was a long-term capital gain!

Bare Bones

Our suggestion for a simplified income tax blank: "How much do you have? Where is it? Send it in."

Progress

Two things are certain—death and taxes. But death doesn't get worse every time Congress meets.

Rainy Days

Taxes are the way the government has of artificially inducing the rainy days nobody has been saving for.

Economics

Death and Taxes ... why can't they come in that order?

Base Salary

An old-time politician was trying to interest a young man in running for a public office. "Look," he said, "It's good for thirty thousand dollars a year." And then he added, "The salary alone is five thousand."

I Knew Him Well

Many years ago there was a congressman from North Carolina named Strange. When he was in his last illness and knew he was not going to recover, he said to his son, "I've decided what I want on my tombstone: 'Here lies an Honest Congressman.'"

"And then your name?" prompted his son.

"No," said the father solemnly, but with a twinkle in his eye, "that won't be necessary. People who read it will say, 'That's Strange.'"

Service

A Hartford delicatessen owner was called in to review his income tax return. "I slave all day to make a living for my wife and two sons," he complained to the IRS agent, "and you question my measly $7,000 income. Why?"

Agent: "It's not your income tax we question. It's the six trips you made to Italy last year, which you deducted as a business expense."

Delicatessen owner: "Oh, that. I forgot to tell you—we also deliver."

Progressive Income Tax

I just read that when Herbert Hoover was President, he gave all his salary back to the government. Now they got us all doing it.

M.D., I.R.S.

Psychiatrists say that it's not good for a man to keep too much to himself, and the Department of Revenue says the same thing.

Pay Off

All of us are working for the government. The trick is to get paid for it.

Significance

In government expenditures—a million bucks is only a drop in the budget.

2 + 2 = 4

Statistics recently released in Washington prove conclusively that ... Washington is full of statistics.

Honesty

Judge: (to alleged chicken thief) "Do the people across the road from you keep chickens?"

Defendant: "They keep some of them."

Progress

Never put off until tomorrow what you can do today. There may be a law against it by that time.

Mumbling

In Cleveland's court of common pleas, a convicted housebreaker recently greeted his penal fate with exhilarated expectation—until the court clerk hastened to correct the judge who had just sentenced him to five years in the Ohio State University.

I Want

Lawyer: "Well, do you want my honest opinion?"

Client: "No, no, I want your professional advice."

Oration

A young lawyer attended the funeral of a millionaire financier. A friend, who arrived at the funeral a little late, took a seat beside the lawyer, and whispered, "How far has the service gone?"

The lawyer nodded towards the clergyman in the pulpit and whispered back tersely, "Just opened for the defense."

Anger

Facing the jury, the judge angrily asked: "What possible excuse can you give for acquitting this man?"

"Insanity, your honor," replied the foreman.

"All twelve of you?" cried the judge.

Mechanic

The judge said to the witness, "Can you corroborate that statement?"

The witness replied, "I can't corroborate that statement, your honor, because my corroborator is flooded."

Discretion

"Did you properly present your bill to the defendant?" the judge asked the plaintiff.

"Yes, sir."

"What did he have to say?"

"He told me to go straight to the devil."

"And what did you do then?"

"I came to see you."

Caustic Rustic

An Anti-Poverty Commission investigator recently checked on a farmer who reportedly was paying his help below standard wages. The farmer willingly introduced him to the hired hands. "This here is Gordon. He milks the cows, works in the fields and gets forty-five dollars a week. And this young lady is Betsy Lou. She cooks and cleans and gets thirty dollars a week, plus room and board."

"Sounds okay so far," said the inspector. "Is there anyone else?"

"Only the half-wit," replied the farmer. "He gets ten dollars a week, tobacco, and room and board."

"I'd like to meet him."

"You're talkin' to him right now," the farmer pointed out crisply.

Profit Sharing

At the scene of an automobile accident, a bum asked one of the victims, "Have the police been here yet?"

"No."

"Has the insurance guy been here yet?"

"No."

Then he asked, "Would you have any objection if I lie down beside you?"

Traveling Salesman

A Scottish traveling salesman, held up in the Orkney Islands by a bad storm, telegraphed to his firm in Aberdeen: "Marooned here by storm, wire instructions."

The reply came: "Start summer vacation as from yesterday."

Ad

Author James Gwaitney's new novel was not selling in Philadelphia so he inserted the following classified ad in the two metropolitan newspapers: "YOUNG MILLIONAIRE, good-looking, wishes to meet with view to matrimony, a girl like the heroine in 'Enduring Young Charms,' Written by James Gwaitney." With 24 hours the book was sold out.

Big Saver

You know what they say: Save a dime here and a dime there and before you know it you'll have twenty cents.

Deficit

Deficit is what you've got when you haven't got as much as you had when you had nothing.

Rainy Day

I've been saving up for a rainy day. So far I've got a pair of dry socks.

Money Isn't Everything

Of course money isn't everything, but it helps you keep in touch with the children.

Handicap

Hobo: "Won't you help a poor, crippled man?"

Man: "You look healthy enough. In what way are you crippled?"

Hobo: "Financially."

It's OK

A young feller just out of school got a job as a teller in a bank. The first day on the job the cashier tossed him a package of bills. "Here," he said, "count these bills and see if there are 100."

The youth started counting. He got up to 58, stopped counting, and threw the package into a drawer. "No sense counting any further," he commented to the cashier. "If it's OK so far, it's probably right all the way."

Employer

An employer is a man who is early when you're late and late when you're early.

Elephant

This is sponsored by the Elephant Moving & Transfer Co. They're slow but they never forget your address.

Ulterior Motives

The boss called one of his employees into the office. "Jones," he said, "I've been watching you. You get in early and leave late. You've never missed a day. You get all your work done and help Smith when he's overloaded; you've never complained and never asked for a raise. Tell me, just what the hell are you up to?"

Federal Aid

A freshman in high school turned in the following explanation of federal aid. Federal aid is the same thing as drawing blood out of your left arm, and putting it into your right arm, while you spill 95% of it on the floor.

No Soap

One of the major soap manufacturers is now producing a new kind of soap. It's hollow in the middle so there are never any little pieces left over.

Siesta

We have a new conference table in our executive offices—it's 8 ft. wide, 30 ft. long—and sleeps 20.

Shoot the Works

A newly rich tycoon was being fitted by an exclusive tailor. "Like a vent in the jacket?" the tailor asked. "Naw," replied the magnate, "I can afford the best, go ahead and put an air-conditioning unit in."

Message

I called my accountant. His secretary said he was out but would be back in 1 to 3 years.

Fish Story

You can tell your dollar bill is counterfeit if the seal of the United States is balancing a fish on his nose.

Gold Brick

The latest statistics reveal that there are 13 million Americans who are not working. And there are even more if you count those with jobs.

Pay As You Go

Nowadays, instead of paying as they go, many people seem to prefer running on ahead and letting it catch up!

Deflation

It's tough to pay a dollar a pound for meat but it's even tougher when you pay half a dollar.

Credit

If you don't want to lose your shirt, don't keep putting things on the cuff.

Hard Work

Uncle Cold Rolled says—Hard work never hurt any-one—who happened to be wealthy enough to hire somebody else to do it.

Reality

I never worry. I've got enough money saved to last me the rest of my life—unless I buy something.

Bewildered

One of the great puzzles in life is ... How a fool and his money got together in the first place.

Budget

Balancing your budget gets worse each year; these days, you just can't reconcile your net income with your gross habits.

A Rainy Day

Save your money. Some day it may be worth some-thing!

Off the Top

How about the executive who bought a wig and charged it to overhead!

Loan

I asked the engineer for a hundred dollars and I said, "Can you lend me a C-note for a month, old boy?"

He said, "Certainly not, what would a month-old boy do with a C-note?"

⅔ of a Dozen

Luke could be a top-notch salesman if he tried. Why, last year, he sold nine top-notches.

Breath Taking

The man who invented life savers made a mint.

Why Not?

If at first you do succeed—it's probably your father's business.

Run Away

I invested and was doing well, 'til the company split. With my money.

Fast Flyer

The dollar doesn't go very far these days, but what it lacks in distance, it makes up in speed.

Plan Ahead

And there's the guy who stole $5,000 worth of groceries and escaped on a motorcycle.

Wooden Nickel

Grab all the wooden nickels you can get. These days the wood is worth at least six cents.

Ten Cent Value

An engineer from Hamilton Standard writes that the dime isn't entirely worthless—it makes a fairly good screwdriver.

Get Well

Postage is so high now—every time you send a get well card you get sick!

A Penny Saved

Grandad saved his first dollar in a ten cent frame. Now, the frame is worth a dollar, and the dollar is worth ten cents.

Rainy Day

The money saved for a rainy day buys a much smaller umbrella nowadays.

Long Life

With medical science doing such a great job of making us live longer, the posterity we're counting on to pay off the national debt may be us!

Last Payment

Customer: "Here's the final installment on the baby's furniture."

Storekeeper: "Splendid. And how's the little fellow getting on?"

Customer: "Wonderfully. He was top man in his high school class last term."

Poor Cat

Inflation affects everyone. Five years ago a neighbor of mine died and left $10,000 to his cat. And today, that cat is broke!

Savings

If the average man saves for the next twenty years at the rate he has been saving for the last six months, he'll be able to retire at age sixty and owe $100,000.

Weightless

I wondered about the astronauts. How weightlessness felt. My wife said, "Like carrying $10 worth of groceries in a shopping bag."

Vegetarian

With today's high cost of meat, the only thing that keeps me from becoming a vegetarian ... is the high cost of vegetables.

Rally

General Window closed slightly higher yesterday.

Adjustment

Sharp rise in National Baseballs after being batted around earlier.

Hot

Mid-Western Fireworks skyrocketed at the final bell.

Flare

Safety Match Corp. enjoyed a short flare of activity.

Grapefruit

On the better side, Texas Grapefruit spurted.

Down

National Casket down six.

Elevator

Mobile Elevator moved in a decided downward trend.

Too Bad

The McBride Road Map Co. has folded.

Pipeline

Pearl Street Edition:
    General Pipeline split today. (I didn't know it was defective).

Drop

Smith Brothers took a drop.

Crash

Community Telephone Pole was hard hit by the automotives.

Alarm

Some alarm was expressed over Household Clock Co.

Film

Expired Film Inc. developed a decidedly negative trend.

Bundle

I lost a bundle in the market yesterday. My shopping bag broke.

Telescope

My brother highly recommended North American Telescope for long range.

Murder

Uncle Stainless made a killing in the market yesterday—shot his broker.

BLOCK BUSTERS

RLS

Water Sport

Did you hear about the Russian who enrolled his son in the Moscow Yacht Club? He wanted to be able to say, "My red son's in the *sail* set."

Pun Fun

A man sent his son to the drugstore to buy a copy of "Of Human Bondage." "Get yourself a soda while you're there," he told his boy. At the drugstore, the kid did as he was told but set the book and soda on the counter. As he wandered through the store, somebody stole them both. The boy started to cry and the owner inquired, "What's the matter, son?"

Through his tears, the boy replied, "I've lost my Maugham and pop!"

Aesop's Tale

Fred, from Stoney Brook, Long Island, would have you believe that long, long ago when Aesop died, he went to Heaven and there became a saintly waiter.

One day, several angels were seated around a table regaling one another with stories when one beckoned to Aesop. "Come on over and tell us a Mother Goose yarn," he called.

"I'm sorry," replied Aesop coldly, "but that's not my fable."

World Series

Jose, a little Mexican boy, saved all his money so he could come to the U.S.A. and see a World Series game. Jose arrived in New York and went to the ticket booth. The man told him, "I'm sorry, kid, but we are sold out for the Series."

"But I have come all the way from Mexico to see a game," pleaded poor Jose.

"Ah, go climb a flag pole," quipped the ticket man.

When Jose arrived home in Mexico, he told his pal, Pedro, what had happened, and Pedro asked, "Did you see the game through?"

"Si," Jose said, "I did what the man said and climbed the flag pole in Yankee Stadium. Oh, but everybody was so nice. They all stood up and looked at me and with a band assisting them, they sang up to me, 'Jose, can you see?"

Subway Scare

A subway inspector named Stein was checking the tracks one day when an unscheduled train suddenly rounded a curve and careened toward him. He sought frantically for a recess in the wall, found one and scrambled into it. And so it was that a niche in time saved Stein.

Small Joke

During a rare outside-of-the-Curtain tour a midget acrobat of the Prague Circus decided to defect. He presented himself to the American Embassy in France and asked: "Pardon, but can you cache a small Czech?"

Poetic License

A pair of hungry poets went into the speedy home furnace installation business, and advertised, "Two Bards That Heat in ¾ Time."

Weather or Not

There was this dinosaur which was so long that while the sun was shining on its nose, it could be raining on its tail. Another creature comes along and says: "Hey Dino—how's the weather in detail?"

Judgment Day

Pat Casey was taken to court for misbehaving and he told the Judge that his good friend Mike Flaherty had fixed it so he wouldn't have to go to jail. The Judge sentenced Pat to ninety days, however, and warned him, "In this Court, I am afraid that Flaherty will get you nowhere."

Wicked Tale

A father sent his two sons into the hills on a cold night to herd sheep. Later he went out to see how they were getting along. He found one son dutifully watching the sheep and asked, "How are you?" "Fine, father," replied the son, "but my lamp has gone out and I am cold." Whereupon the father gave the boy a new wick for his lamp.

The father then came upon the second son who was fast asleep under a tree. He woke him and asked, "How are you?" The boy replied, "I am cold, father, and need a new wick for my lamp." The father shook his head and said, "You shall not have it. There is no wick for the rested."

Mixed Drinks

Each evening the doctor arrived at his favorite bar at the same time and ordered a chestnut daiquiri. So, the bartender would make his drink just before he arrived. One night, as the bartender began to mix the chestnut daiquiri, he discovered he was out of chestnuts. Worried, he searched high and low. Finally he found an old wizened hickory nut. Thinking quickly, the bartender ground up the hickory nut and sprinkled it over the daiquiri. The doctor arrived, took one sip of his drink, looked at the bartender, and said, "This isn't a chestnut daiquiri." "No," the bartender answered. "It's a hickory daiquiri, Doc!"

Get the Point?

R.B.B. Jr. from Bloomfield asks:
Have you heard about the Tate compass? It was the world's cheapest compass and thousands were sold to hunters and trappers all over the north woods. Unfortunately, the Tate's compass was also the worst in the world. Some needles pointed south, some east, some anywhere. This gave rise to the well-known expression "He who has-a-tates is lost."

Boots Away

Roy Rogers had just bought himself a brand new pair of snazzy cowboy boots for $600 and, understandably, was very proud of them. However, before they were a week old, they were inadvertently left out overnight, on the veranda of his sprawling ranch house in the California mountains. Wouldn't you know a pesky mountain lion that had been ravaging area farms and ranches, would come along on a moonless night and tear one of those new boots to shreds? He did exactly that and Roy was fit to be tied. Gazing at the ripped-up boot with tears in his eyes, Roy grabbed his Winchester, jumped on Trigger and took off for the mountains in the customary cloud of dust, vowing to bring in the carcass of that *#*#*censored*#*#* feline marauder. To make a long story short, he succeeded. Hours later, when Roy's wife, Dale, saw her hubby riding through the gate with the dead lion slung across Trigger's rump, she called out, "Pardon me, Roy. Is that the cat that chewed your new shoe?"

Remember the legendary Mill Famey?

The greatest pitcher I ever faced? Millard Fillmore Famey of the Sioux City Scouts. A super relief pitcher, he threw nothing but strikes and needed no warmup! Being so terrific he enjoyed certain privileges. He could drink beer in the dugout or even right out on the mound if he felt like it. In the 1929 championship game we were behind 2-0 in the bottom of the ninth. The Sioux City pitcher suddenly weakened and loaded the bases on three dinky hits with none out! Famey was summoned. He finished one beer in the dugout and brought another with him to the pitching rubber, drained the can and dropped it near the mound. A bit tipsy, he walked three batters on twelve pitches, forcing in three runs and giving us the victory 3-2. As I ran across the field to our dressing room I noticed this shiny object near the pitcher's box, picked it up and showed it to one of my jubilant teammates who was rushing by. I said, "Look at this, would you? What the heck is it?" He studied it for a quick moment and said, "Why ... that's the beer that made Mill Famey WALK US!"

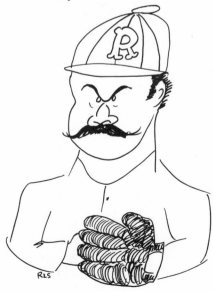

The Lion and Albert
by Marriott Edgar (1932)

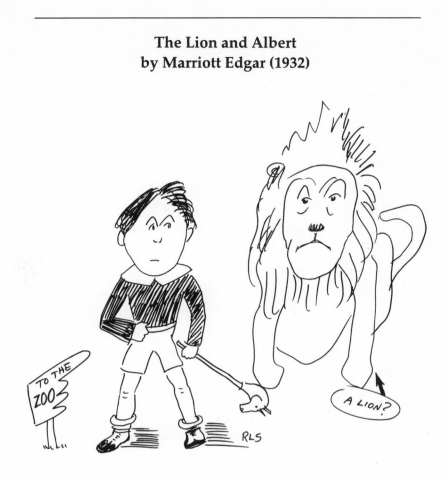

There's a famous seaside place called Blackpool,
   That's noted for fresh air and fun,
And Mr. and Mrs. Ramsbottom
   Went there with young Albert, their son.

A grand little lad was young Albert,
   All dressed in his best; quite a swell
With a stick with an 'orse's 'ead 'andle,
   The finest that Woolworth's could sell.

They didn't think much to the Ocean:
   The waves, they was fiddlin' and small,
There was no wrecks and nobody drownded,
   Fact, nothing to laugh at at all.

So, seeking for further amusement,
  They paid and went into the Zoo,
Where they'd Lions and Tigers and Camels,
  And old ale and sandwiches too.

There were one great big Lion called Wallace;
  His nose were all covered with scars—
He lay in a somnolent posture.
  With the side of his face on the bars.

Now Albert had heard about Lions,
  How they was ferocious and wild—
To see Wallace lying so peaceful,
  Well, it didn't seem right to the child.

So straightway the brave little feller,
  Not showing a morsel of fear,
Took his stick with its 'orse's 'ead 'andle
  And pushed it in Wallace's ear.

You could see that the Lion didn't like it,
  For giving a kind of a roll,
He pulled Albert inside the cage with 'im,
  And swallowed the little lad 'ole.

Then Pa, who had seen the occurrence,
  And didn't know what to do next,
Said, 'Mother! Yon Lion's 'et Albert,'
  And Mother said, 'Well, I am vexed!'

Then Mr. and Mrs. Ramsbottom—
  Quite rightly, when all's said and done—
Complained to the Animal keeper,
  That the Lion had eaten their son.

The keeper was quite nice about it;
  He said, 'What a nasty mishap.
Are you sure that it's *your* boy he's eaten?'
  Pa said, 'Am I sure? There's his cap!'

The manager had to be sent for.
  He came and he said 'What's to do?'

Pa said, 'Yon Lion's 'et Albert,'
  And 'im in his Sunday clothes, too.'
Then Mother said, 'Right's right, young feller;
  I think it's a shame and a sin,
For a lion to go and eat Albert,
  And after we've paid to come in.'

The manager wanted no trouble,
  He took out his purse right away,
Saying, 'How much to settle the matter?'
  And Pa said, 'What do you usually pay?'
But Mother had turned a bit awkward
  When she thought where her Albert had gone.

She said 'No! someone's got to be summonsed'—
  So that was decided upon.

Then off they went to the P'lice Station,
  In front of the Magistrate chap
They told 'im what happened to Albert,
  And proved it by showing his cap.

The Magistrate gave his opinion
  That no one was really to blame
And he said that he hoped the Ramsbottoms
  Would have further sons to their name.

At that Mother got proper blazing,
  'And thank you, sir, kindly,' said she.
'What waste all our lives raising children
  To feed ruddy Lions? Not me!'

The Return of Albert
(Albert Comes Back)
by Marriott Edgar (1934)

You've 'eard 'ow young Albert Ramsbottom,
  In the Zoo up at Blackpool one year,
With a stick and 'orse's 'ead 'andle,
  Gave a lion a poke in the ear.

The name of the lion was Wallace,
  The poke in the ear made 'im wild;
And before you could say, 'Bob's your Uncle,'
  E'd up and 'e'd swallered the child.

'E were sorry the moment 'e'd done it,
  With children 'e'd always been chums,
And besides, 'e'd no teeth in 'is noddle,
  And 'e couldn't chew Albert on t'gums.

'E could feel the lad moving inside 'im,
  As 'e lay on 'is bed of dried ferns,
And it might 'ave been little lad's birthday,
  'E wished 'im such 'appy returns.

But Albert kept kicking and fighting,
  Till Wallace arose feeling bad,
And felt it were time that 'e started to stage
  A come-back for the lad.

So with 'is 'ead down in a corner.
  On 'is front paws 'e started to walk,
And 'e coughed and 'e sneezed and 'e gargled,
  Till Albert shot out like a cork.

Old Wallace felt better direc'ly,
  And 'is figure once more became lean,
But the only difference with Albert
  Was 'is face and 'is 'ands were quite clean.

Meanwhile Mister and Missus Ramsbottom
  'Ad gon 'ome to tea feeling blue;
Ma says, 'I feel down in the mouth like,'

Pa says, 'Aye! I bet Albert does too.'
Said Ma, 'It just goes for to show yer
    That the future is never revealed,
If I thought we was going to lose 'im
    I'd 'ave not 'ad 'is boots soled and 'eeled.'

'Let's look on the bright side,' said Father.
    'What can't be 'elped must be endured,
Every cloud 'as a silvery lining.
    And we did 'ave young Albert insured.'

A knock at the door came that moment,
    As Father these kind words did speak,
'Twas the man from t'Prudential,
    E'd called for their 'tuppence per person per week.'

When Father saw who 'ad been knocking,
    'E laughed and 'e kept laughing so,
That the young man said, 'What's there to laugh at?'
    Pa said, 'You'll laugh an' all when you know.'

'Excuse 'im for laughing,' said Mother,
    'But really things 'appen so strange,
Our Albert's been ate by a lion,
    You've got to pay us for a change.'

Said the young feller from the Prudential,
    'Now, come come, let's understand this,
You don't mean to say that you've lost 'im?'
    Ma says, 'Oh, no! we *know* where 'e is.'

When the young man 'ad 'eard all the details,
    A bag from 'is pocket he drew,
And 'e paid them with 'rest and bonus,
    The sum of nine pounds four and two.

Pa 'ad scarce got 'is 'and on the money,
    When a face at the window they see,
And Mother says, 'Eeh! look, it's Albert,'
    And Father says, 'Aye, it *would* be.'

Young Albert came in all excited,
　　And started 'is story to give,
And Pa says, 'I'll never trust lions again,
　　Not as long as I live.'

The young feller from the Prudential
　　To pick up the money began,
And Father says, 'Eeh! just a moment,
Don't be in a hurry, young man.'

Then giving young Albert a shilling,
　　He said, 'Pop off back to the Zoo.
'Ere's yer stick with the 'orse's 'ead 'andle,
　　Go and see what the Tigers can do!'

RLS ON LIFE AFTER MARRIAGE

RLS

Clever

"What do you think would go well with these new red slacks?" asked the beaming wife.

Her husband surveyed the scene, then replied, "How about an ankle-length coat?"

Apprehension

My wife told me, "Get a good night's sleep. I've got something to tell you in the morning."

Duck

A listener from Old Lyme writes: A shivering wife in the back of a rowboat said to her duck-hunting husband, "Tell me again how much fun we're having. I forgot."

Quite

Two solemn-looking men were riding together in a New York-New Haven and Hartford car passing through Wallingford.

First: "Is your wife entertaining this week?"
Second: "Not very."

Cooperation

A conscientious father was advising his son who was about to get married. "Cooperation is the foundation of a successful marriage," the father said solemnly. "You must do everything together. If your wife wants to go for a walk, go for a walk with her. If she wants to go to the movies, go the movies with her. If she wants to do the dishes, do the dishes with her."

The son listened dutifully and then asked, "Suppose she wants to mop the floor?"

A Spray in Time

My wife is so tender hearted she uses hair spray on bugs. It doesn't kill 'em—it just keeps 'em in their place.

Desperation

She said, "Pretend I'm a bartender and talk to me."

Gone

He: "Last night you said there was something about me that you liked."

She: "There was, but you spent it all."

Logic

My wife doesn't care how good looking my secretary is—as long as he's efficient.

An Occident

Show me a man who comes home in the evening, is greeted by a smile, is encouraged to take off his shoes, has pillows arranged on the floor for him, and is served a delicious meal—and I'll show you a man who lives in a Japanese restaurant.

Balanced

She won't mend his socks because he won't buy her a new mink coat. If he doesn't give a wrap, she doesn't give a darn.

Not Presentable

"Did you say you want a divorce on the ground that your husband is careless about his appearance?"

"Yes, He hasn't been home in nearly two years."

Tick-Tock

"Is your husband very good at repairing things around the house?"

"Well, I don't like to criticize, but ever since he fixed the clock the cuckoo backs out and asks, 'What time is it?'"

Up-to-Date

A refugee couple arrived in the U.S. After long study, they finally passed their examinations and their citizenship papers arrived in the mail. The husband rushed into the kitchen with the news: "Anna, Anna," he shouted, "At last we are Americans!"

"That's fine," she replied, "now you wash the dishes."

Life Saver

Tomorrow is Valentine's Day. Don't forget to get your wife a present or there may be another massacre.

Inventory

"Will you tell the court what passed between you and your wife during the quarrel?" asked the judge. The long-suffering husband replied: "A flatiron, a rolling pin, six plates and a teakettle."

A Fine System

A woman listener in Cobalt writes that she never lies about her age. She always says she's as old as her husband—then she lies about his age.

Reminiscing

One man says he'd like to go back to the days when his wife's meals were carefully thought out instead of carefully thawed out.

Memories

A New Haven newspaper reported that a generous gentleman had donated a new loudspeaker to his church in fond memory of his wife.

The Easy Way

The banker was plainly exasperated with the man opposite him at the desk. "Your finances are in terrible shape," he said. "Overdrawn accounts, extended loans— why do you allow your wife to spend more money than you make?"

"Frankly," the man replied with a sigh, "because I'd rather argue with you than with her."

Right Now!

"What can I do about this terrible toothache?" the suffering victim asked his friend. "Well," said the friend, "When I have a toothache, I go to my wife, she puts her arms around me and caresses and comforts me, and the toothache seems to go away." "Wonderful!" exclaimed the victim, "is she home now?"

Finis

A listener claims that the following notice appeared on the society pages of a Fairfield County newspaper: "Norman Smith and Cynthia Jones were married last Saturday, thus ending a friendship that began in grammar school."

Accuracy

The best 10 years of a woman's life is between 29 and 30.

Expensive Roll

My wife's got a vehicle that costs me $200 a mile! A shopping cart!

Body Language

First She: "Does your husband talk in his sleep?"

Second She: "No, and it's terribly exasperating. He just grins."

Good Try

The little woman had spent the whole afternoon and made a real effort to balance her checkbook. When her husband came home, she handed him four neatly typed sheets, with items and costs in their respective columns. He read them over carefully: "Milkman, $11.25, cleaners, $4.67, etc." Everything was clear except one item reading "ESP $24.49."

Warily he asked, "What does ESP mean?"

She explained, "Error some place."

Charm

At a social gathering in Washington, a young man was asked by the lady seated next to him to guess her age. It was apparent that he was a member of the diplomatic corps from his answer. "I have an approximate idea," he said, "but I can't decide whether to guess 10 years younger on account of your looks or 10 years older on account of your brain."

Cheroot

A husband won't have to admit he's henpecked, if he smokes a big, black cigar as he washes the dishes!

The End

The honeymoon is over when the dog brings you your slippers and your wife barks at you.

Culinary Tip

Remember, you spoon when you date ... but you fork-over when you're married.

SSHHHH!

The husband tiptoed in at 4 a.m. and his wife caught him at the door.

"So," she said triumphantly, "home is the best place after all."

"Nope," he said sourly, "it's just the only place that's open."

Clumsy

"How is your wife?" the man asked a friend he hadn't seen for years.

"She's in heaven," replied the friend.

"Oh, I'm sorry," This didn't sound quite right so he said, "I mean, I'm glad." That was worse yet, so finally he came out with, "Well, I'm surprised."

Defeat

He took defeat like a man—blamed it on his wife.

Tip Toe

Man (at police station): "Could I see the burglar who broke into our house last night?"

Sergeant: "Why do you want to see him?"

Man: "I'd like to ask him how he got in without waking my wife."

At Ease

Plumber: "I understand you have something here that doesn't work."

Housewife: "Yes. he's in the living room lying on the couch."

Aha!

The husband came home one night and proudly announced to his wife that he had bought himself a hearing-aid.

"Well, thank goodness," said his wife. "That's what I've been telling you to do for the past eight years."

"Oh!" the husband laughed. "So that's what it was."

Good Fortune

"I'm a self-made man."

"You are lucky. I am the revised work of a wife and three daughters."

Testy

Here's a card from a listener in Torrington. He says his wife is the kind of woman who goes through life wanting to see the manager.

The Answer

A lady in West Haven has a solution to hubby's snoring problem. Separate rooms. She sleeps on the couch ... he sleeps in a motel in New Jersey.

Pow!

Wife: "I just set my hair."

Husband: "What time does it go off?"

Impossible

Only a wife could ask, "Don't turn around—but who is that couple that just came in?"

I Get No Respect

"My husband was named Man-of-the-Year."

"Well, that shows you what kind of a year it has been."

Control Yourself

R.W. in Westport writes that he told his wife, "Let's put it this way, you're an addict ... and our grocer is a pusher."

Point of View

Big, strong men make docile husbands. So do big, strong women.

Really?

A fellow who works at Sikorsky writes that he told his wife, "You're overdrawn." She said that was crazy ... she still had four checks left in her checkbook.

Of Course

My wife can remember every tiny detail about our wedding—except why she married me.

Lessons

Marriage teaches you loyalty, forbearance, self-restraint, meekness and a lot of other qualities you wouldn't need if you stayed single.

Balanced

A man and his wife walk into a marriage counselor's office. She talks for 10 minutes and then says, "That's my side of the story. Now let me tell you his."

Learning

He married a wisp of a girl, then he learned the will of the wisp.

A Sport

Got my wife a new clothes dryer. 200 feet of rope.

No, Sir

A couple from Shelton were visiting friends, talking about married life, and how they got along together. He said, "My wife and I haven't agreed on anything in the last ten years." She says, "Twelve years!"

One Way

There's only one way to win an argument with your wife. However, nobody knows what it is.

It Rhymes

Their joint account's retarded by one persistent flaw. He's fast on the deposit, but she's faster on the draw.

Late, Late

"What is your husband's average income?"
  "Oh, about midnight."

Caution

Note from a friend in New Britain—it's a warning, is what it is. He says: "Let me caution you and your listeners. If you are out on the streets of New Britain today, be extra careful ... my wife is teaching my mother-in-law how to drive."

Colorful

I gave my wife her first driving lesson today. I said, "Now, baby, stop on red, go on green, and pull over to the side of the road when I turn pale."

Generosity

My wife wanted something to drive so I bought her a hammer and some nails.

Progress

Wife: "I couldn't fix your supper, dear, the electricity is off."

Hubby: "But we have a gas stove."

Wife: "Yes, but we have an electric can opener."

Insight

A woman shopping in G. Fox was looking over thermometers. "I'll take that Fahrenheit one—I know that's a good brand."

Surprise!

Then there was the lady from Canaan who wondered where her husband spent his evenings—until she came home early one night and there he was!

New Model

Wife: "I've changed my mind."

Husband: "Thank heavens. Does it work better now?"

Hardly Ever

Somebody once asked Justice Felix Frankfurter why Supreme Court judges never perform weddings, and he replied, "I guess it's because marriage isn't considered a federal offense."

Ready to Go

The nice thing about drive-in movies is that you know where your wife's shoes are when you get ready to go home.

Samaritan

"You look tired."

"I am. I've been all over town trying to get something for my husband."

"Had any offers?"

Good Fortune

Conversation in a Waterbury bar: "I was real lucky on my wedding day. I got a wife and a cigarette lighter and they both work."

Switch

You never realize how much a person's voice can change until your wife stops yelling at you and answers the phone.

Definition

Courtship is the process of seeking a girl's hand until she has you under her thumb.

Advice

If you don't like the way women drive ... stay off the sidewalk.

I Think

Timid man to wife: "We're not going out tonight and that's semi-final."

Limit

A fellow took his girl to Ocean Beach and spent $8. That was all she had.

Tempting

Wife: "I baked two kinds of biscuits today. Would you like to take your pick?"

Husband: "No, thank you. I'll use my hammer."

Humph

The Mona Lisa—the picture that looks like your wife does when you say you had to work late at the office.

BOB ON CHILDREN, TEENS, AND ELDERS

AND THEN, IN 1872 ....

Little League

A friend of mine in East Hartford has a son who just became a Little League football player, and the guy's wife is worrying her head off. She's afraid the kid may be traded or sold.

Bundles

A mother, her arms filled with bundles, got on the bus with her five-year-old daughter. The girl paid the two fares, then, feeling some explanation to the driver was necessary, said in a clear strong voice, "I'm paying the fare today because my mother is loaded."

Under A Bed

A small boy had been naughty and had been reprimanded. His mother told him he must take a whipping. He fled upstairs and hid in a far corner under a bed.

When the father came home, the mother told him what had happened. He went upstairs and proceeded to crawl under the bed toward the youngster.

Excitedly the boy whispered, "Hello Pop, is she after you too?"

Cabbages

A father called in his seven-year-old daughter and explained that her mother had found a lovely little sister early that morning among the cabbages.

"Now," he said, "you write your brother Jack (away in the Army) and tell him about it.

The child wrote the letter and gave it to her father to mail. The parent couldn't resist peeking to read her childish explanation.

"Dear Jack," the letter read, "it's a girl. You owe me a buck."

Shoe Shine

Sign on the side of a Hartford shoeshine boy's stand: "Regular shine, ten cents. Deluxe shine with wild flapping sounds, 25 cents."

Youth

To many modern parents, youth is stranger than fiction.

Sleepy Time

Did you know that there are two things that can sleep standing up? Horses and fathers with month-old babies.

Generation Gap

No wonder there's a generation gap and children don't understand parents. Parents make you go to bed when you're not sleepy ... and make you get up when you are.

Outdoor Project

Father brought home logs for the fireplace in the trunk of the family car and, as he was unloading them, his 4-year-old son asked, "What are you gonna do, Dad ... build a tree?"

Eskimo Query

An Eskimo mother was sitting in the igloo and reading from a story book to her small son. "Little Jack Horner," she read, "sat in a corner."

"Mother," asked the kid, "what's a corner?"

Large Problem

Doc asked my brother if he had any trouble with his ears or nose. Kid said, they were always in the way when he took off his T-shirt.

Lightening

A Westport father was driving his little girl home from a birthday party during a nasty thunderstorm. She asked from the back seat, "Daddy, who's taking all those pictures?"

Picture Windows

Architects designed picture windows to bring the outdoors into a home, but all you really need is a couple of small children.

School Days

Once again the doors of the nation's schools have swung open, amid cheers from thousands of bright-eyed eager ... mothers.

Lost

Sorrowfully, the little boy looked up and down the street, then went to the policeman on the corner. "Sir," he asked hopefully, "did you see a lady go by without me?"

Cleanliness

Our pretty new grade school teacher asked her class, "Cleanliness is next to what?"

One boy quickly answered, "Impossible."

Ping-Pong

My kids gave me half a ping-pong table for my birthday. All I can play is ping.

Mosquitoes

Mosquitoes are like little children; the moment they stop making noises, you know they're getting into something.

Musical

A couple visiting New York City decided to take their 12-year-old son to a hit musical for his birthday.

They began to feel a little uneasy during the opening number when a line of chorus girls appeared clad only in scanty green and white ribbons.

As the dance ended, the boy leaned over and whispered to his mother, "Mom, did you see that?"

"Did I see what?" the mother asked apprehensively.

"Those girls," exclaimed her son, "They're wearing our school colors."

Violin Practice

Father listened to his seven-year-old scratch away on his violin while the hound dog howled dismally nearby. As the practice session wore on, the father asked the boy, "Can't you play something the dog doesn't know?"

Truth Revealed

"I dragged my son to the barber shop to get some of that ridiculous hair cut off," a man was telling a friend, "and he turned out to be the neighbor's kid."

Brownie

Four-year-old sister: "When I grow up I'm going to be a Brownie."

Three-year-old brother: "When I grow up I'm going to be a peanut butter and jelly sandwich."

Math Test

Lad in the fourth grade who can't seem to get the hang of long division left all the answer spaces blank on a recent test paper but printed in neat, square letters across the bottom of the sheet, "I can spell chrysanthemum."

Confusing

Being a kid is no fun. If you're loud they punish you ...
If you're quiet they take your temperature.

Choosy

The mother of five-year-old Nancy told her if she didn't
eat more the doctor would have to give her liver shots.

"I don't want liver shots," Nancy fussed, "but I'll
take hamburger shots."

Secret

If you don't believe a ten-year-old boy can keep a secret,
ask him where he left the family hammer.

Writing Lesson

Almost every child would learn to write sooner if he
was allowed to do his homework on wet cement.

Galloping

Mama Tucker hates to be disturbed when she is watching her favorite TV program, and is particularly aroused
when her neighbor's unruly flock of kids start dashing
around her backyard. The other evening they went gal-
loping through her kitchen. "Do that again," she yelled
after them, "and I'll call the police!"

One of the kids yelled back, "Who do you think is
after us now?"

Camp Notes

Last summer he got a letter from his kid at camp ...
"Dear Dad, wish you were here ... instead of me."

Hands On

Parents nowadays should give their children a free hand
... often, and in the right place!

Inspiration

A teacher from Bolton writes: I had just told my third
grade arithmetic class that the next day we would begin

carrying numbers in addition examples, when a little boy solemnly declared, "Miss Watson, I may not be able to carry too much; I haven't been feeling so strong lately."

Prayers

At bedtime, a little fellow got down on his knees and began saying his prayers. When he was finished he began asking God for the things he wanted for Christmas. He called them out one by one in a particularly loud voice. His mother said, "You don't need to shout. God isn't deaf."

"I know," he said, "but gran'ma is."

Fussy Eater?

A mother reported to relatives that her baby was now eating solids—mainly newspapers, rubber bands, bugs and pencils.

Ice Cream

An eight-year-old came home with an ice cream cone in each hand. His mother asked him how much he had spent. He told her that he hadn't spent anything.

"Did someone treat you?" she asked.

"No."

"Did you steal them?"

"No."

"Then how did you get them without spending your money?" the mother wanted to know.

"I told the girl at the ice cream place to give me a chocolate cone in this hand and a maplenut cone in this hand," he explained, "and then I told her to reach in my pocket for my money—but be careful not to disturb my pet snake."

City Slicker

E. W. from Springfield writes us about a three-year-old boy who went for an automobile ride. When he came home his aunt asked him what he saw. The boy said he saw a black and white cow sitting down chewing gum.

Scared

The floor nurse at Saint Francis Hospital was trying to speak to a patient in the children's ward via the intercom, but received no answer.

"Jimmy, I know you're there," she said into the microphone.

After a few seconds, a tiny, quavering voice replied: "What do you want, wall?"

Sure Thing

Any boy who is eager to mow the lawn ... is too young to.

Porthole

A little boy came down to the docks with his parents to greet his big brother who was returning from overseas duty. In the confusion, the parents couldn't see their favorite soldier, but somehow the youngster managed to pick him out. "There he is!" the boy shouted, pointing up at the big transport.

"Where?" demanded the father.

The youngster pointed to a porthole high in the side of the ship. "Up there," he said, "with the boat around his neck!"

Chicks

During a nature class the teacher began telling her third grade pupils about the chicken. "Isn't it wonderful," she exclaimed, "how little chickens get out of their shells?"

One of her eight-year-old charges was moved to respond, "What beats me is how they get in."

He Tried

The Sunday-school class was composed of three-year-olds. The teacher asked: "Do any of you remember who St. Matthew was?" No answer.

"Well, who was St. Mark?" Still no answer.

"Surely someone must remember who Peter was?"

The little faces were full of interest, but the room was quiet. Finally, a tiny voice came from the back of the room.

"I fink he was a wabbit."

Question

Science is trying to find the answers to such questions as why a kid cannot walk around a puddle.

Mendelian Law

How do we know that parenthood is hereditary?

If your parents don't have children, you won't either.

Starting

We know how the doctor slaps a newborn baby to make him cry, but what does he do to make him quit?

Static

A boy is a restless noise with dirt on it.

Teaching

Have you heard about the kindergarten for gamblers' children? They are taught to count 8, 9, 10, Jack, Queen, King, Ace.

Togetherness

Children keep a family together ... especially if they can't find a baby-sitter.

Dieting

Junior (age 4): "I'm going on a diet, mommy, so I won't be wanting any more green vegetables."

Peek-A-Boo

There was a dear little pink baby on the train and the elderly man stopped to peek-a-boo at it.

"A fine youngster," said he to the young mother. "I hope you will bring him up to be an upright and conscientious man."

"Yes," smiled the fond mother, "but I'm afraid it's going to be a bit difficult, as ..."

"Oh, nonsense," continued the adviser; "as the twig is bent so is the tree inclined."

"I know it," agreed the mother. "But this twig is bent on being a girl, and we are inclined to let it go at that."

Cautious

Ad in a classified section: "FOR SALE, cheap. Well-used Beatle albums. If a young woman answers, hang up and call back later."

Control

"I hear that the Allens are separated," said Mrs. Spineless.

"Yes," replied her husband, "and Mr. Allen signed a legal document giving her the control of their children."

"Oh, John!" sighed Mrs. Spineless, "I wish we could get a document that would give us control of our children."

Smart Move

Kids: The best way to get a puppy dog is to ask your mommy for a baby sister.

Cranky

Tommy came home from school one day all excited. He happily explained to his mother that the class had a magic record player at school. Said little Tommy, "You don't even have to plug it in to electricity .... We just crank the handle, and it plays by itself."

Heave Ho

When it came time to go home from school the teacher had to help the children into their galoshes. After pulling and tugging on 30 pairs she came to the last child, Michael. When she had finally got his galoshes on him, he said, "You know, teacher, these aren't mine."

THROUGH THE STEELE YEARS
YEARS
A Photo Album

Bob at outset of his career at WTIC in 1936. Yes, that's a microphone.

Robert L. and Robert H. about to take a spin on Bob's Indian motorcycle (1939).

Bob hawks newspapers (Hartford Times) *at corner of Main and Asylum. He had agreed to the stunt if one of his sports predictions should bomb. It bombed. (1945)*

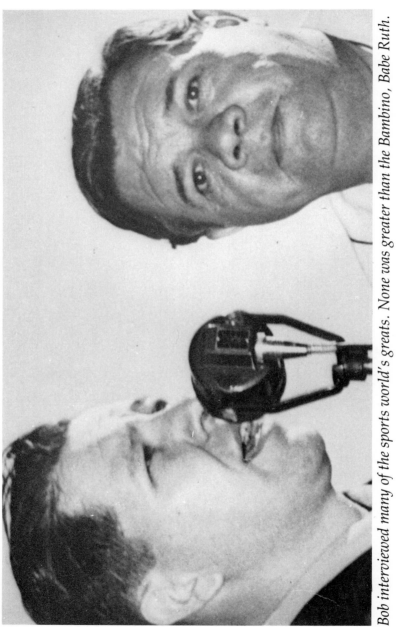

Bob interviewed many of the sports world's greats. None was greater than the Bambino, Babe Ruth.

WTIC announcers in "The Good Old Days" (about 1946). Front row, L-R, Ed Anderson, Bob, Bruce Kern, Dick Westerkamp. Back row, L-R, Ross Miller, Bob Tyrol, Floyd Richards, Jim Strong.

A couple of Bob's good friends, the late Paul W. Morency, President of WTIC, and former Connecticut Governor John N. Dempsey, salute Bob for his 25 yrs. at WTIC. (1961)

Bob & Jean Colbert, the winners in the 1963 street sweeping contest kicking off Hartford's Spring Cleanup Drive.

"But gee whiz, officer, I was going to be late at the studio."

Bob imparts advice to Muhammad Ali day before first Joe Frazier bout. Ali says it sounds good to him. The following night Ali lost to Frazier in 15 rounds!

Listeners often ask Bob, "Where do you get your jokes?" Here's the answer. His four sons make up his entire staff of writers. Left to right: Paul, Philip, Robert and Steven, shown early in their careers.

Bob and wife, Shirley, celebrate son Robert's landslide victory in 1972, returning him to Congress for a second term.

Two Bobs discuss joke before Steele introduces Hope at Hartford Civic Center (Oct. 1975).

Bob at the voting booth in Wethersfield the day son Robert battled Ella Grasso for Connecticut Governorship (Nov. 1976). Guess who Bob voted for!

"The word for the day is 'pachyderm.'" (1977)

Bob sells ties for the Heart Fund at Civic Center. (1978)

Bob says, "Good morning, Jadies and Lentlemen" at 5:30 a.m. from his huge round table in 19th floor studio.

The harassed woman groaned, sat the boy down, grabbed hold of his feet and struggled until she succeeded in getting the galoshes off.

"Now then, who do these belong to?" she asked.

"My brother," explained the boy, "but my mother makes me wear them."

Richard Who?

From Hamden comes the story of the little tyke who rushed home from school and asked his mother, "Who is Richard Stands?" Said the little fellow, "He must be important. Every day at school we say, 'I pledge allegiance to the flag of the United States of America and to the Republic for Richard Stands'."

Opening Day

On the opening day of school ...

Eighteen million mothers gravely watched their solemn youngsters leave home. Gratefully, they sighed, "God bless school."

Two million, eight hundred thousand teachers commented, "There must be an easier way to earn a living."

Eighty-four percent of the new kindergartners vowed, "I'm not going to school today, tomorrow, or ever!"

Three million dogs whimpered and whined at bus stops.

Help!

Five-year-old Sally rushed into the kitchen and asked, "Daddy, what time is it when the big hand is on seven and the little hand is on the floor?"

Disappearing Act

One small boy to another as they were coming down an escalator: "I wonder what happens when the basement is full of steps."

Legislation

"I want you to understand," said the teacher, "that it is the law of gravity that keeps us on this earth."

"Please, Miss Krimminhagen," asked little Nellie, "how did we stick on before the law was passed?"

Etiquette

A kindergarten teacher in Longmeadow was instructing the youngsters in her class as to proper classroom etiquette.

"If anyone must go to the bathroom during the day, please raise your hand," the teacher requested.

"How does that help?" asked one of her students.

Come Back!

Two Boy Scouts, whose younger brother had fallen into the lake, rushed home to mother with tears in their eyes. "We're trying to give him artificial respiration," one of them sobbed, "but he keeps getting up and walking away!"

Crowded

His mother said, "I demand that you put on a fresh pair of socks every day!" He promised he would. By the end of three weeks he couldn't get his shoes on!

Description

The class had a lesson on Eskimos and was asked to describe them. One bright youngster began: "The Eskimos are God's frozen people."

Lament

Lament of a teenage daughter's parent: "It seems like only yesterday she took her thumb out of her mouth and stuck her finger in the phone dial.

Growing Up

Many a teenager is growing up to be the kind of kid his parents wouldn't let him play with.

Aptitude

A Newtown father says his teenage son took a job-aptitude test—was found to be best suited for retirement.

Burglars

A neighbor said that he thinks burglars broke into his teenage daughter's room and ransacked it, "but it's hard to tell."

Manners

The headmaster of an exclusive prep school looked aghast when one of the new boys was caught wiping his fork on the tablecloth.

"Rogers!" he thundered. "Is that what you do at home?"

"Oh, no sir," Rogers answered politely. "At home we have clean forks."

Future

"I hear you have a boy in college. Is he going to become a doctor, an engineer, or a lawyer, perhaps?" The slow, quizzical answer was: "Right now the big question is: Is he going to become a sophomore?"

Mail

The easiest way to get a letter from your son or daughter in college is to write one yourself saying, "Enclosed find check"—and don't enclose the check.

Complaint

My father complains that he spent $25,000 on my college education, and all he ever got was a quarterback.

Freshman

A rooming house landlord received a phone call from the mother of a college freshman. "Please keep an eye on Albert for me," begged his mother. "See that he gets plenty of sleep and doesn't drink or run around too much.

"You see," she added, in an apprehensive tone, "this is the first time he's been away from home—except for two years in the Marines."

Confession

Confessions to a bartender: "I feel a little foolish when I realize that the son I wouldn't trust with my old Studebaker is now flying a million-dollar jet for the Air Force."

Protest

One way to stop student protesting would be to make it a required course.

Evidence

From circumstantial evidence, such as a damp bath towel, and an occasional step on the stairs, the people in the second house from the corner are pretty sure their son is home from college.

Professor

Professor: "Why is a well-ordered schoolroom like a Ford?"

Bright Freshie: "Easy! Because the crank's up in front."

Professor: "Yes, but there's more to it than that. The crank's up in front, and all the nuts are in their proper places."

Gift

It used to be that when a fella really liked a girl, he gave her his class ring. Nowadays, he lets her use his hair curlers.

Invention

A farmer visited his son's college. Watching students in a chemistry class, he was told they were looking for a universal solvent.

"What's that?" asked the farmer.

"A fluid that will dissolve anything."

"That's a great idea," agreed the farmer. "When you find it, what are you going to keep it in?"

Money

Father to son asking for money: "Junior, have you ever considered being a professional fund raiser?"

Who's First?

The preacher had just united two hippies in holy wedlock. He looked at them in puzzlement and then asked, "Will one of you please kiss the bride?"

Pharmacists

Old pharmacists never die—they just count themselves out.

Salesmen

Old salesmen never die—they just get out of commission.

Burglars

Old burglars never die—they just steal away.

Gamblers

Old dice shooters never die—they just fade away.

Gardeners

Old gardeners never die—they just spade away.

Fishermen

Old fisherman never die—they just smell that way.

Truck Drivers

Old truck drivers never die—they just can't make the grade.

STEELE'S SIGNS AND SYNONYMS

Church

Sign on a church: COME IN AND HAVE YOUR FAITH LIFTED!

Lodge Hall

Sign on a lodge bulletin board announcing a pot-luck dinner: "All members are reminded to bring their wives and one hot dish."

Newsroom

Sign in a radio newsroom: "Our Weather Bureau is a Non-Prophet Agency."

Garden Shop

Sign in a garden store: "Please be seeded."

Clock Shop

Card in the window of clock shop: "There's no present like the time."

Antique Shop

Sign on a bird bath at an antique shop: "FOR SALE: Cheep."

Retreat

A retired math professor hung this sign on his mountain retreat: "After Math."

Muffler Shop

Sign in a muffler shop: "Our job is exhausting."

School

Traffic sign in front of school: "Drive slowly. Some of our youngsters are not angels and we want to keep them that way."

Hat Shop

Sign on a hat store in New Delhi: TURBAN RENEWAL.

Hot Dog Stand

The owner of a hot dog stand on the Berlin Turnpike is a thorough believer in the old adage that "frankness" is a virtue. He has a large sign hanging on his stand which reads, "Don't make fun of our coffee. You may be old and weak yourself some time."

Kennel

A kennel in Litchfield advertised dachshund puppies for sale with the sign ... git a *long* little doggie.

Boutique

Two convivial friends were wending their way along Pratt St. about 2 a.m., when one of them stopped to gaze dazedly at a sign.

"Whatchu lookin' at?" said the other.

"That sign."

"Whazzit say?"

"Ladies' Ready to Wear Clothes."

"Dern near time, if anyone was to ask me," came the reply.

Wet Day

Sign for a wet day: "You are urged to burn your toast while the hazard is low."

University

This sign was seen above a row of hooks in a cloakroom in one of the large universities. "For Faculty Members Only." Scribbled below it was: "May also be used for Hats and Coats."

Pawn Shop

Sign in a pawnshop opposite Broadcast House—"Hock it to me."

Hardware Store

Sign in a hardware store: "Our bug spray will make your ants yell uncle."

Car

I saw this bumper sticker the other day: "Pass me. I'm a student."

Clothing Store

Sign on Joe's Clothing store: "Fire Sale—Featuring Smoked Herringbone Suits."

Dance Hall

Sign in a dance hall: "Good Clean Dancing Every Night Except Sunday."

Advertising Agency

Sign in an advertising agency: "A good ad should be like a good sermon: It must not only comfort the afflicted—it must also afflict the comfortable."

Butcher Shop

A sign on a butcher shop in London proclaims proudly: "We make sausage for Queen Elizabeth." On a rival shop across the street is another sign: "God save the Queen."

Church

The First United Methodist Church of Oakhurst, N.J. has a sign in front that has attracted considerable attention. It says: "Come to Ch--ch! What is missing?"

The obvious answer is "You Are."

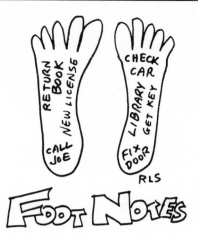

Beer

Sign of our times, seen over a hot dog and beer place: "Frank 'N Stein."

Loan Office

Sign in a loan office: "Now you can borrow enough to get completely out of debt!"

Shoe Repair

A shoe repair shop had a big sign, advertising several styles of rubber heels, with a picture of a beautiful girl saying, "I'm in love with America's No. 1 heel."

Underneath in small feminine handwriting was this addition: "Too bad, sister. I've already married him."

Classified

Here's an ad in the classifieds: "Phonograph for sale: needs minor repairs, needs minor repairs, needs minor repairs ..."

Adult Western

Adult Western: A movie in which the cowboy loves his horse, but he's sorta worried about it.

Forgery

Forgery: When a man has to make a name for himself.

Quicksilver

Quicksilver: What the Lone Ranger used to say when he was in a hurry.

Swimming Pool

Swimming Pool: A crowd of people with water in it.

Cannibal Cookbook

Cannibal Cookbook: A thousand and one ways to serve humanity.

Mini-Strone

Mini-strone: A very small cup of soup.

Pedestrian

Pedestrian: A man who didn't believe his wife when she told him the family needed two cars.

Middle Age

Middle Age: That time of life when your narrow waist and broad mind change places.

Commercial Traveler

Commercial traveler: A man who goes to the refrigerator during the sponsor's message.

Sponge Cake

Sponge cake: Any cake you make by *borrowing* all the ingredients.

Optimist

Optimist: A fellow of eighty who marries and goes house-hunting in a good school district.

Fanatic

Fanatic: Someone who is highly enthusiastic about something in which you aren't remotely interested.

Pessimist

Pessimist: Someone who complains of the noise when opportunity knocks.

Subtlety

Subtlety: The art of saying what you think and getting out of range before it is understood.

Junk

Junk: Anything that lies around in your way for ten years and you throw it away two weeks before you need it.

Nonchalance

Nonchalance: The ability to look like an owl when you've acted like a jackass.

Bore

Bore: Someone who goes right on talking while you're interrupting.

Optimist

Optimist: A guy who falls off a balcony on the 20th floor and, as he passes the 10th floor, says, "So far, so good!"

Pedestrian

Pedestrian: A motorist who has finally found a parking place.

Auction

Auction sale: Where you get something for nodding.

Hippie

Hippie: Looks like Tarzan, dresses like Jane and smells like Cheetah.

Girdle

Girdle manufacturer: Another fellow who lives off the fat of the land.

Newspaper

Newspaper: A portable screen behind which a man hides from the woman who is standing up in a bus.

Stalemate

Stalemate: A husband who keeps telling the same jokes.

Mason and Dixon

Mason & Dixon's Line: The boundary between "you all" and "youse guys."

Fan Belt

Fan belt: What some guys take to a football game in a flask.

Locomotive

Locomotive: A crazy reason for doing something.

Laplander

Laplander: A clumsy person on a crowded bus.

Genealogy

Genealogy: Tracing yourself back to people better than you are.

Dry Doc

Dry Doc: Non-drinking physician.

Adolescent

Adolescent: A youngster old enough to dress himself if he could just remember where he dropped his clothes.

Divorce

Divorce: A suit that takes you to the cleaners.

Upper Crust

Upper Crust: A handful of crumbs held together by a wad of dough.

Diplomat

Diplomat: A guy who thinks twice before saying nothing.

POOR BOB'S ALMANAC

Galoshes

Nothing angers the man who wears galoshes and gets a cold more than having a neighbor who doesn't and doesn't.

Even Handed

It's not whether you win or lose but how you place the blame.

Old Belchertown Adage

Never slap a man's face while he's chewing tobacco.

Choice

Better to become bent from hard work than to become crooked from avoiding it!

On the Other Hand

To forget your other troubles—try wearing tight shoes.

Idea

If you keep an open mind, someone might drop in a worthwhile thought.

Share and Share Alike

The guy who keeps telling you you can't take it with you is planning on taking it with him.

Tightfisted

A bird in the hand makes it difficult to pick up a wheelbarrow.

Shifty

Always forgive your enemies. Nothing annoys them more!

From a Listener

The next time you're discouraged and feeling mighty blue, take a look at the mighty oak and see what a nut can do.

Fuller Explanation

"They told me, by golly, it couldn't be done ... with a smile I went right to it ... and tackled the thing that couldn't be done ...and, by golly, I couldn't do it!"

Taboo

Very few people realize it, but did you know you can steam clams by making fun of their religion?

What a Bunch

Time flies like the wind, but fruit flies like bananas!

I.Q.

As a thought for the day, a man from Meriden offers the following for your edification and amusement: The intelligent man that says, "It can't be done," should stay out of the way of the idiot that's doing it.

Safety First

Are you suffering from painful sunburn? This is not a commercial. With your eyes wide open, turn your head to the left and look back over your shoulder as far as possible. Repeat this to your right and continue this as often as you feel it's necessary. This exercise won't do your sunburn any good, but at least no one can sneak up and slap you on the back.

Writer's Cramp

A reporter once asked William Faulkner, "What is the most important thing you've learned from 35 years of writing?" Faulkner replied, "Never set your coffee cup where it can spill on your newly-typed manuscript."

Bad Connection

The bathtub was invented about 1850, the telephone in 1875. One listener has figured out that if you had been living in 1850, you could have sat soaking peacefully in your tub for 25 years before the phone rang.

Experience

A person becomes wise by observing carefully what happens when he isn't.

Heavy

Hard of hearing is tough—but being hard of thinking is a good deal worse.

Quiet Please!

If you want the world to beat a path to your door, just lie down and try to take a nice quiet nap!

Now or Never

I have found this to be true: You can get anything you want in life ... if you wait until you don't need it.

Which Way to the Egress?

Some people get lost in thought because it's unfamiliar territory.

Get Rich Quick

Think of a product that costs a dime to make, sells for a dollar, and is habit-forming.

Heady Remark

Old age is simply a case of mind over matter. If you don't mind ... it doesn't matter.

Martial Arts

To protect yourself from muggers, go to a Kung Fu school ... and stay there!

Old Adage

Remember: A friend in need is a friend to avoid.

By Product

Trouble is usually produced by those who produce nothing else.

Slippery

Some folks butter you up to put the bite on you.

Odds On

Don't forget friends ... you get TWO years to pay. And FIVE if you don't.

Sky's the Limit

Confucius, or somebody, say, "People who go around with their heads in the clouds, will never go as high up as people with their *feet on the ground.*"

No Smudges

A man never knows how careful he can be until he wears white flannel pants and white shoes.

Pull

Today, many young men find their best vocational aptitudes exist in fields where their fathers hold influential positions.

Fact or Fiction?

Student: "It says here that if we study hard, don't drink, smoke or run around with girls we'll live longer. Is that true?"

Professor: "We won't know for sure until somebody tries it."

Cut Up

Any stubborn stain can be removed with a pair of scissors.

Hear, Hear!

Best after dinner speech: "I'll take the check."

Lapse

The human brain is a wonderful thing. It starts working the moment you are born and never stops until you stand up to speak in public.

Make It Brief

To make a long story short, there's nothing like having the person you're talking about walk into the room.

Mystery

Keep smiling, and everybody will wonder what you are up to.

Never Noticed

Men occasionally stumble over the truth, but most of them pick themselves up and hurry on as if nothing had happened.

Don't Look at Me

Medical science says that whisky cannot cure the common cold, but then neither can medical science.

Catchy

Why is it that disease is contagious but health isn't? Wouldn't it be nice if it could be the other way around? Imagine being able to catch good health from somebody, or being able to spread good health around. Just think of being healthy and getting into a crowded elevator with several sick people. You sneeze and everybody gets well. That thought came to me in a dream last night.

Try It

Many years ago Mahatma Gandhi was interviewed by reporters on a mission to London. One of them asked, "What do you think of Western Civilization?"

Gandhi smiled faintly and answered,"I think it would be a very good idea."

In the Know

Sudden thought: Only one man in a million understands the international situation. Isn't it amazing how we keep running into him?

Wish You Were Here

A real friend is somebody who takes a winter vacation on a sun-drenched beach somewhere and *doesn't* send a card.

Brevity

Recipe for a good speech: Add shortening!

Are We There Yet?

The perfect place for a picnic is often a little farther on.

Duck

At railroad crossing ... Here's how to figger; In case of a tie ... The engine's bigger.

Back to the Drawing Board

The brotherhood of man has been turning out too few brothers and too many hoods.

Steady

"I love you when you're good," a father told his small daughter. The little girl answered quickly: "I love you *all* the time, Daddy."

How Come?

There are three kinds of people: The few who make things happen, the many who watch things happen, and the big majority who have no idea what has happened.

Take What You Can

Mark Twain's home overflowed with books. When a close friend commented about the lack of shelf space and the dozens of books stacked on desks and windowsills at his library, the great wit remarked: "Well, you know how difficult it is to borrow book cases?"

Useful

You can do a lot with an old house these days if you are handy with money.

Guaranteed

Nothing lasts as long as a necktie you don't like.

Balancing Act

You are getting old if it takes you longer to rest than it did to get tired.

The Little Things

Have you ever noticed that a girl will scream at the sight of a mouse, yet sit right down beside a wolf?

Cosmetology

Time, the great healer, is also a very poor beautician.

Easy Come, Easy Go

She went to a Chinese Beauty Parlor. An hour later she was ugly again.

LETTERS TO STEELE
FROM ALL OVER

Tropical

A man owned a farm on the Bolton-Manchester border, which border was constantly under dispute. Once it was in Bolton and the next time in Manchester. Finally the farmer decided to have the land surveyed. After the surveyor had finished, he said to the farmer, "Well, I am happy to report that your farm is in Manchester.

"Thank goodness," said the farmer, "I don't think I could have stood another one of those Bolton winters."

Watch It

A ship sank off New London with a cargo of clocks. All hands were lost.

Hikers

There are two kinds of people in Czechoslovakia, optimists and pessimists. The optimists think that the entire Czechoslovak people will be transported to Siberia. The pessimists believe they will have to walk.

Gesundheit

A Martian watched a man at a slot machine in Las Vegas. The player hit the jackpot. While the cherries, pears, and peaches spun around, the machine shook and sputtered and delivered an outpouring of coins. The Martian stepped up to the slot machine and said in a voice of concern, "Baby, you ought to do something for that cold."

And An Udder

Letter from Windsor: Dear Boo—er, Bob, Our cow died so we don't need your bull any more!

Ordinary Life

The life insurance salesman from Travelers, a perfervid fellow, was giving his best to the prospect. At the moment of quoting the price he said, "The cost of this policy is only $20 a month. That's the cost of straight life. That's what you want, isn't it."

"Well," admitted the prospect, "I guess it is. Only I'd like to have a little fun on Saturday nights."

Big Deal

I played cards in Las Vegas once—and I'm a very practical gambler, I only lose what I think I can afford. Last night I thought I could afford my car and house.

Orient

Did you hear about the new Chinese Cocktail Lounge on Asylum Street? It's called the Taiwan-On.

Spicy

A fellow from Windsor wants to go to the Thousand Islands. A wealthy man, he has a salad dressing plantation.

Hugger Mugger

To get away from the crime and violence of New York, he moved to Arizona where he was attacked by a mugger with asthma.

Regards

"When you were in Switzerland did you see the Alps?"

"Yes, a wonderful family."

Cut Up

Letter from home: "Dear Son: Your father has a new job. He has 500 people under him. He cuts the grass at the cemetery—Mother."

Smooth

A woman in Bristol writes that she has dreams about being with Kojak ... running her fingers thru his hat.

Milestone

A Longmeadow man writes he's celebrating today—his son has finally grown out of the old man's shirts.

Quebec

In Quebec a U.S. tourist struggled with a French restaurant menu. "Nous voulons," he stammered, "deux consomme avec bread and butter ... that's beurre and something or other. Comprenez?"

The waiter shrugged. "Sorry. I come from Boston and I don't know a word of French."

"Well then," snapped the tourist, "get me somebody who does!"

Nasty Turn

In Idaho a hotel burned down. The firemen were on the job, but they couldn't get their hose through the revolving door.

Watch It

I took First Prize in the Best-Dressed Men in Hartford contest. 'Course when they learned it was missing they made me put it back.

Turnabout

Hiram went to New York determined to make his fortune pulling some skin games on innocent strangers. However, the first fellow he tried to sell the Brooklyn Bridge to turned out to be the owner, and if he hadn't paid him ten dollars to keep quiet, the man would have had him arrested.

Jet Lag

A fellow in Canton described his European trip: Breakfast in London, dinner in New York, luggage in Rio.

Optional

An Englishman on a visit to the West decided to go horseback riding. The cowboy who was to attend him asked, "Do you prefer an English saddle or a Western?"

"What's the difference?" he asked.

"The Western saddle has a horn," replied the attendant.

"I don't think I'll need the horn," said the Englishman. "I don't intend to ride in heavy traffic."

Trio

An Englishman, and Irishman, and an American were flying low over the Sahara Desert.

"Beastly place!" said the Englishman.

"The devil's home," said the Irishman.

"What a parking lot!" said the American.

Crocked

People think I am a human encyclopedia—they ask so many odd questions. I had a letter yesterday from a woman in Ridgefield wanting to know why she doesn't see or hear about Betty Crocker any more.

She went stir crazy.

Isn't It Obvious

How can you tell a boy's nationality by introducing him to a girl? Easy. An English boy shakes her hand; a French boy kisses her hand; an American boy asks her for a date; a Russian boy wires to Moscow for instructions.

Bagged

I never will forget the first day I arrived in New York and for the first time, stepped on the street of dreams, Broadway. I looked up at the buildings towering above me and shouted, "I'm going to conquer you! Do you hear me? I'm going to conquer you!"

Then I looked down and discovered my bags were gone.

Aunt Bessemer

The Aunt Bessemer Look-Alike Contest will be held Monday. The Winner will get $5,000 worth of plastic surgery.

Avid Reader

A lady from Vernon received a thank-you note from a 9-year-old nephew: "I love my book you sent me at Christmas. I have been reading it day and night and am now on page eight."

Soup

A lady from Higganum says, "The average waiter walks 12 miles a day. No wonder my soup is always cold when I get it."

Weeds

A dentist from Vernon didn't know how bad his grass was until he applied weed killer and in two hours his whole lawn was gone!

Propaganda

A friend in Haddam has some advice for those worried about inflation, "All this talk about the high cost of living is just propaganda put out by people who pay rent, doctor bills and groceries."

Roundup

A listener from Moodus says his Dad was with the FBI in Chicago ... That's where they caught him.

Cash Flow

MLR from East Hartford complains that cold cash melts away when you are having a hot time.

Progress

A woman from Newington asked me, "What did you do before you got into radio?"

"I was a seam straightener in a liverwurst factory."

Exit

A fellow from Enfield writes, "I know a fella who put on his Nehru jacket; his wife put on her sari; two hours later something fascinating happened. They were deported!"

ROBERT LEE STEELE
AND THE AUTOMOBILE

RLS

Fair Enough

Things even out. We've got most of the cars ... Russia has most of the parking space.

Math

Automotive arithmetic—The number of horn blasts in a traffic jam is equal to the sum of the squares behind the wheels.

Population Explosion

And a tip to the pedestrians. By 1985 there will be 200 million automobiles. If you want to cross the street do it now.

Bumper Crop

If all the cars on I-84 were placed bumper to bumper some idiot would try to pass them.

Time Warp

Each year it seems to take less time to fly across the ocean and longer to drive to work.

Faster

I was driving along in the morning traffic on I-91 and saw a guy walking. I asked him if he wanted a lift and he said no, he was in a hurry.

Overreaction

A young lady teacher from New Canaan was halted by a YIELD sign on her way north. Right behind her was a cab driver. The traffic was fairly heavy and the young lady didn't move fast enough for the cabby. He leaned out of his seat and yelled, "The sign says 'yield,' lady, not 'surrender'."

Appearance

The officer pulled the motorist to the side of the road and exclaimed, "When I saw you come zooming around that curve I said to myself, 45 at least!"

"Well, you're wrong, officer," protested the woman driver. "This hat just makes me look older."

Silence

He got hit by the library bookmobile. As he was lying there screaming, the lady driver leaned out and said, "Shhhhh."

Batteries

Woman drive to gas station—asks attendant, "Do you charge batteries here?" He said, "We certainly do, Ma'am." She says, "Well, put a new one in this car and charge it to my husband!"

Right on Red

We'll discuss the average woman. Who is she? Where is she heading? And why didn't she signal?

Get Up and Go

If you think the younger generation isn't interested in getting ahead, just wait'll one of 'em pulls up next to you at a stop light.

Questionable

A garage man answered the distress call of a woman motorist whose car had stalled. He made an examination and informed her it was out of gas.

"Will it hurt the car," she asked, "if I drive home with the gas tank empty?"

Pedal

At the license bureau they asked my wife ... "How many feet are required to stop a car traveling 30 mph?" She said, "Two ... one for the brake and one for the clutch."

Wild

"Call the service station!"

"Why?"

"Tell them that the tiger they put in my gas tank ate up my muffler."

Serendipity

"It's not just the work I enjoy," said the Ansonia taxi driver. "It's the people I run into."

They're Off!

The parking meter is a device that bets $2 to your dime that you can't get back before the red flag pops up.

Conservation

Fat Pedestrian (knocked down by a car): "Couldn't you have gone around me?"

Motorist: "I wasn't sure whether I had enough gas left."

Bird's Eye View

The sports car owner was giving a friend his first ride in one of the low-slung models. The friend appeared to be puzzled, so the driver asked what was wrong. "I can't figure out what that long wall is which we've been passing."

"That's no wall," snapped the driver, "it's the curb."

Relativity

Happiness is doing 80 in a 70 mph zone and a police car passes you doing 90 chasing a guy doing 100.

Good Ole Ways

No, they don't make cars the way they used to, and it's a good thing. Who'd want running-boards and kerosene tailights ... and a crank to get it started ... and manually operated windshield wipers?

Radio Controlled

I'm not sorry I got into radio. It's easier than parking cars.

Crank

The only thing a cranky person is good for is starting a 1911 Ford.

No Parking

"At last, we finally found a parking space." "Yes, but I wonder what town this is?"

Exercise

I've been on a kind of exercise kick lately. You know, get up early and go ride my bike about for about an hour. It's really great. 'Course, bike riding has taught me one advantage to riding in a car. When you pass a skunk ... you can ROLL UP THE WINDOW!!

Lethal

What part of an automobile kills the most people? The nut behind the wheel.

My, My!

Oh, that's a shame! It says here that due to the new high speeds on the highways today, Burma Shave would have to put their signs further apart.

Tourists

We can only hope that tourists from abroad will not be unduly shocked by the shoddiness of our motor cars. Apparently they are so badly put together that most motorists feel they must hold the top on while they drive.

Car Buyer

Prospective car buyer: "You mean that little compact costs $8,500? Why, that's almost the price of a big car."

Salesman: "Well, sir, if you want economy, you've got to pay for it."

Moving Violation

Frequent naps will keep you from getting old—especially if taken while driving.

Effective

You see these signs on the highway: "Stop, Look and Listen!" The only time I ever saw a driver stop, look and listen, was when there was something wrong with his motor.

Choice

The new 1975 Nin-Cum comes as a Sedan or Coupe. He chose the Nin-Cum-Coupe.

Amen

If all the automobiles in the USA were placed end to end, it would be Sunday afternoon.

Watch Out

A frayed tire is a tire to be afraid of!

NUTS AND BOLTS—
A STEELE COLLECTION

Q & A

Q. My soil is washing away too fast for good grass to take hold. A neighbor says I should try some rye? What do you think?

A. I think you should hold off the drinking till you solve your grass problem.

Q. I don't want to uproot any good plants in my garden, but I don't know how to tell the weeds. What do you recommend?

A. Don't tell them at all; sneak up and yank is my motto.

Q. I'm looking for something robust and hardy to creep over my fence. Any ideas?

A. I should say so, and I'll be right over!

Q. I cannot tell a sprout from a sprig. What's the difference?

A. That's what I say.

Woody Plant

A fussy woman who had been peppering the nursery-man with many questions, finally asked: "What would you suggest for a spot that gets only a little moisture, is clay soil on a rocky ledge, which the morning sun beats down upon—and the afternoon sun never gets to?"

"Lady," snapped the nurseryman, "how about a nice flagpole?"

Camouflage

Well, winter is just around the corner and with it—all that wonderful snow. Oh yes, I really like snow. As the fellow says, it's the only time of the year when *my* lawn looks as good as my neighbor's.

Drip

Give the average husband a few tools and in no time a dripping faucet will be a running stream.

Woodsman, Scare that Tree

Charles and Barbara Ray planted a magnolia tree in their yard 12 years ago but were disappointed because it had never produced even a single bloom over the years.

Barbara heard that if one were to "scare" a tree that it might start producing blooms. The Rays and their children, acting during the darkness of night in order that the neighbors would not think them crazy, began beating the trunk. They were careful not to scar the bark, but the gentle beating continued for some time. This year hundreds of buds appeared and the tree produced gorgeous white blossoms.

Thrifty

There are many, many ways to grow roses. Some people favor a rich loam. Them there are those who insist a mixture of redwood shavings and sawdust is best. And there are groups that advocate a mixture of both. They are known as shavings and loam associations.

Electronic

Newest gadget for homeowners is a radio-controlled lawn mower-snow blower ... only trouble is mine had a defect ... it cut my snow, and threw my lawn all over the neighborhood.

Wanted

What can you tell me about Creeping Red Fescue?

"Lock your doors and windows. Far as I know, he's still at large."

Close

A Rocky Hill listener says: "Anyone who runs a power lawn mower before noon on Sunday should have to *shave* with it."

Good Advice

Two farmers met on the road in Goshen and pulled up.

"Si, I've got a mule with distemper. What'd ye give that one of yours when he had it?"

"Turpentine. Giddap."

A week later they met again.

"Say, Si, I gave my mule turpentine and it killed him."

"Killed mine, too. Giddap."

Dog Food

I had a job at the dog pound in Plainville ... serving soup to mutts.

Cow Conversation

Two cows were grazing alongside the highway down which ran tank trucks of milk on their way to the distributor. On the side of the trucks one could read: "Pasteurized, homogenized, standardized, Vitamin A added." One cow turned to the other and said, "Makes you feel sort of inadequate, doesn't it?"

Surprise Guest

When he answered the doorbell, the man discovered an old friend and a very large dog waiting on the porch. "Come right in, come right in!" he exclaimed.

The friend entered the living room and sat down, while the canine promptly put the man's cat to flight, knocked over a table lamp and several vases, and finally made himself comfortable in an easy chair.

When the guest rose to leave, the host said with a touch of sarcasm in his voice. "Aren't you forgetting your dog?"

"Dog? I have no dog. I thought he was yours."

Fish

One fish says to another, "Hi! How's it going?"

The other says, "I can't complain. I'm keeping my head below water!"

Wood Pigeon

Cross a carrier pigeon with a woodpecker. Not only carries messages but will knock on the door when it arrives.

Turtles

There are no statistics available on the subject ... but I would like to know, how many turtles have fallen in love with army helmets?

Dog

A guy from Torrington sits down on a park bench where a woman is sitting with a dog curled up at her feet.

Guy says: "Does your dog bite?"

Woman: "No."

Guy pets the dog and almost loses his hand. Says to the woman: "I thought you said your dog doesn't bite."

Woman says: "That's not my dog."

Horse

How do you shoe a horse?

You just say, "Go 'way, horse."

Special Delivery

I have just come out with a new dog food that is going to sell like wild fire. Dogs are going to eat it up. I call it "Postman's Heel".

Of Course

"Oh, what a funny looking cow," the chic young thing from Greenwich said to the farmer. "But why hasn't it any horns?"

"There are many reasons," the farmer replied, "why a cow does not have horns. Some do not have them until late in life. Others are dehorned, while still other breeds are not supposed to have horns. This cow does not have horns because it is a horse."

Snake

Me: A snake snapped at me.

You: Snakes don't snap. They HISS!

Me: This was a GARTER snake!

Racer

A little ant was racing 'round and round' a medium sized cracker box. His pal, another ant, observing the first ant, couldn't understand what the furious hurry was. So, he asked his running friend, "Just what's your hurry, pal?" The first ant replied, "Well, there's a sign here that says, 'Tear along the dotted line.'"

Me Too

That lazy rooster never crowed in his life. He always waits for another rooster to crow and then he nods his head.

Stickler

A man crossed a porcupine with a gorilla. I don't know what he got, but it sure gets a seat on the subway.

Cat and Mouse

Customer: When I bought this cat you said it was good for mice. It doesn't even go near them.

Clerk: Well, isn't that good for mice?

Needs Sale

A friend's dog bit my leg.

Did you put anything on it?

No, he liked it the way it was!

Character Sketch

A locomotive struck and killed a cow that had wandered onto the tracks. A section foreman was asked to fill out the accident forms. He did well until he reached the final question: "Disposition of the carcass."

He wrote: "I would have to believe that she was kind of gentle."

Party Time

Kid (at riding academy): "I wish to rent a horse."

Groom: "How long?"

Kid: "The longest you've got, there will be five of us going."

Pig Skin

About the pig swallowing the ball ... it became an inside-the-pork home run.

Hog Fact

Hogs love to scratch themselves and spend most of their waking hours doing so. For their right side they always use their right hind foot, doing a fast circular "rock and roll" to keep from falling. As a result the right ham is muscular and tough.

No one has ever seen hogs use their left hind foot to scratch. For their left side they always rub against a tree or a fence. As a result, the left ham is smooth and tender.

Humble Bee

Do you know why bees hum?

Because they don't know the words.

I.O.U.

A Navy recruit lost his rifle on the firing range. When told that he'd have to pay for it, he protested: "Suppose I was driving a Navy jeep and somebody stole it. Would I have to pay for that too?" He was informed that he would have to pay for all government property he lost.

"Now," the recruit said, "I know why the captain always goes down with his ship."

Names

A flyer sent his son a puppy. They named it "Lightening", but after two days they decided to call it P-47.

Classified Information

A GI clerk in the Quartermaster Corps received waves of documents in the course of his work. One day an Army form came his way; he initialed it and passed it along to the officer for whom it was intended. Promptly, the form came back with this note attached:

"This document did not concern you. Please erase your initials and initial the erasure." (Signed) Lt. S. Hannibal.

Lineup

Like in the Army ... his sergeant told him to go stand at the end of the line. He came back and said, "There's already someone there."

Paratroopers

Asked the recruit, "How many successful jumps do we have to make before we graduate?"

Replied the Sergeant, "All of them son, all of them."

Flat Feet

Medical officer, after examing a mountaineer volunteering for service: "Sorry, we can't take you. You have flat feet, and they couldn't take it. You wouldn't be able to walk five miles."

Mountaineer: "That's too bad. 'Cause I just walked 50 miles to get here and I shore does hate to walk back again."

Peashooter

"Sir, the enemy soldiers are before us as thick as peas."

"All right, shell them!"

George Washington

"George Washington," said the fashion expert's child, "was first in war, first in peace and first to wear a wig and white stretch pants with boots."

Conquerors

Diligent historians, on this date in 1066, the Saxons are conquered by the Normans, also the Freds, Irvings and the Charlies.

Luncheon

A Middletown hotel served 2 private luncheons one noontime, one to a group of clergymen and the other to a group of wholesale liquor dealers. The liquor dealers ordered a special dessert, watermelon soaked with brandy, rum, and Benedictine. The manager of the hotel discovered to his horror that there had been a mix-up and the spiked melon had been served to the ministers.

"What did they say?" he asked the headwaiter. "Were there many complaints?"

"They didn't say a word," the man reported. "They were too busy putting the seeds in their pockets."

Unemployment

Two nuns, eager to learn the way such things are done, accompanied a woman friend to the State Employment Office in Bridgeport to observe her file a claim for unemployment compensation. Pat O'Hara, also in the claims line, rubbed his eyes and looked twice when he saw the nuns. It was too much for him: "Glory be to God," he exclaimed, "business must be bad ... even the Pope is laying them off!"

Chandelier

The Pastor of a little old church in New Milford wanted some improvements, so he suggested a chandelier. This met with some opposition. When he asked his Parishioners why they opposed, came this reply!

"Well," said a spokesman, "First, no one can spell it, so how can we order it? Second, no one can play it if we do get it, and third, what we really need around here is more light!!"

Angel

A visiting preacher knocked on the door of the home of a member of his congregation.

"Is that you, angel?" someone inside called.

"No," replied the minister, "but I'm from the same department."

And the Bishop Obliged

The dear vicar's wife had just died, and as a consequence he wished to be relieved of his duties for the weekend, so he sent the following message to his bishop:

"I regret to inform you that my wife has just died, and I should be obliged if you could send me a substitute for the weekend."

Literary Question

A minister was writing in his study when his little daughter came in. "What are you writing, daddy?" she asked.

"I'm writing a sermon, my pet."

"How do you know what to write?" she asked.

"God tells me," said her father gravely.

After watching her father a few minutes the child remarked, "If God tells you what to write, daddy, why do you scratch some of it out after you write it?"

Sign of the Times

A sign in front of a church read: "You must pay for your sins." Underneath someone added: "If you have already paid, please ignore this reminder."

Vatican

The Vatican had a little difficulty finding a new Pope. No one wants to work on Sundays anymore.

Constitution

Besides being rather a wild youth, Sam Smithers was exceedingly egotistical. A couple of days after he returned from overseas he strolled into a grocery store, where the prohibition amendment was under discussion.

"How about it, Sam?" asked a friend. "Are you peeved because they made the country dry while you were gone?"

Sam drew himself up proudly and gazed at the group of loafers.

"Peeved, nothing!" he ejaculated. "I'm proud of it. Why, they had to amend the Constitution of the United States of America to reform me, and they knew it had to be done when I wasn't here to prevent it."

Well Supplied

Went on a camping trip with the guys this past weekend. We didn't take much equipment. Just 2 bottles of whiskey for snake bites ... and 2 snakes.

Waterbed

Take a waterbed, fill it with beer and you get a foam mattress.

Lecture

Cop: "What're you doing on the streets at this hour?"

Drunk: "I'm going to a lecture."

Cop: "You won't find any lectures around here at 3 a.m."

Drunk: "Wanna bet? Follow me home!"

Still Counting

The number of drunks in this country is *staggering!*

Fill 'er Up

It has been estimated that about a fifth of the cost of a car goes into the engine, but the cost piles up when another fifth goes into the driver.

What a Loss!

Officer McGinty testifying as to the intoxicated condition of the defendant:

"There's no doubt of it, I saw him put a penny in the patrol box at Sixth and Mulberry, then look up at the clock on the courthouse and shout, 'My gosh, I've losht 'leven pounds.'"

Car Thieves

A man telephoned the police to report that thieves had been at work on his car.

"They've stolen the steering wheel, the accelerator, the clutch pedal and the dashboard," he complained.

The police sergeant said he would investigate and hung up. Then the telephone rang again.

"Don't bother," said the same voice, this time with a hiccup. "I got into the back seat by mistake."

Tall 'n Cold

A man walked into a Bristol bar, sat on a stool and said to the bartender, "Give me something tall, cold and full of gin." The man on the next stool drew himself up straight and said, "Sir, I'll have you know you are speaking of the woman I married."

Statistical Insight

An item in the news today says National Car Loadings are down 11%. Consumption of alcohol is up 30%. More people are getting loaded than boxcars!

Kentucky Bourbon

An oldtimer from Kentucky drank two quarts of high-proof bourbon every day of his adult life and lived to be 90. At his cremation it took three days to put out the fire.

Gasahol

My brother-in-law can start a car by breathing into the carburetor.

Real Thirsty

Social worker (visiting Somer's prison): "Was it your love for drink that brought you here?"

Convict: "Gosh no, lady, you can't get nothin' like that in here."

Bottled Sunshine

Orange juice is a health drink. If you will drink one bottle every day for 1,200 months, you'll live to be a hundred years old.

Aches and Pains

Played touch football with some kids. Boy, I'm stiff this morning. I haven't been this stiff since last New Year's Eve.

Recipe

The crack about the Manhattan reminds me of the Charles Dickens Martini—without Olive or Twist.

Medical Dialogue

Doctor: "They tell me you're a hard drinker."

Patient: "Don't you believe it, Doc. It isn't a bit hard."

Beer on Tap

There's a new beer on the market called Beethoven ... it's for people who don't like Bock.

A 1971 RLS
CHRISTMAS CARD

STRANGLED EGGS
AND
OTHER RECIPES

My Favorite

Break two eggs in a bowl, add a dash of cream (Oh! throw the shells away) and a smidgin of cottage cheese. Beat well with a fork but *never* put in blender. (Goodness!) Pour into buttered skillet and cook over medium heat. Push the mixture around to prevent sticking and when it's done the way you like it—moist, dry or in between—you have STRANGLED EGGS A LA STEELE.

Don't Watch the Pot

How to boil water, advice for new brides and other novices:

Take a pan, just about any size will do, but let's use, say, a two-quart pan, if this is the first time for you.

If you've never boiled water before, you won't want to overdo it and yet you'll want to boil enough to make it worthwhile, to have a feeling of accomplishment.

Now, with the pan in your left hand, so you'll have the right hand free to turn the faucet handle (I presume you are right-handed, if you're left-handed, just reverse this), turn on the hot water. (This is a little trick that I stumbled on to some years ago. I have found hot water will boil quicker than cold water, no matter what day of the week it is.)

Now fill the pan to within an inch and a half of the top. No need to get a tape measure, just use your judgment.

Place the pan of water over any burner that is not in use (careful, don't spill). Now turn on the heat. Whether you use gas or electricity you will need heat. If you have a lid for the pan, that will help speed up the boiling.

Now just step back and stand around or sit down, or do as you like. I think everyone has his own favorite way of waiting for water to boil.

But remember this, don't watch it while you are waiting because it will never boil.

RLS

RLS

Lefse (Pronounced Leff'-suh)

5	cups mashed potatoes
¼	cup cream
2	teasp salt
1	stick margarine or butter
2½	cups flour

Mix cream, salt and margarine with mashed potatoes. Cool thoroughly. Add flour and mix. Make into small patties and roll out very thin. (Keep rest of dough cold until needed.) If the dough is difficult to roll, add a little more flour. Fry in melted shortening till brown, turning once. You can butter it and sprinkle with powdered sugar if you like. It's okay by me. Or you can cover it with jam and roll it up. Or you can call your neighbor over and let her figure out what to do with it.

Mock Crabmeat Salad

2	cups raw shredded parsnips
1	cup finely sliced celery
1	tbsp. chopped pimiento
½	cup. quartered ripe olives
½	cup mayonnaise (homemade if possible)
1	tbsp. lemon juice (fresh)
2	tsp. finely sliced green onion
¾	tsp. salt or to taste

Mix parsnips, celery, pimiento & olives. Blend mayonnaise, lemon juice, onion and salt. Add to parsnip mixture and toss. Refrigerate for 2-3 hours. You'll think you're eating crabmeat.

BOB CLOSES
THE PROGRAM

Eggzactly

Thank you for listening to old Uncle Boob ... er, Bob. I must hasten away—I've got a date with an egg and I don't want to break it.

A Tip

Thanks for listening. 'Til Monday morning, the best to you and yours. This is Merging Traffic. Watch out for me on the highways.

Have A ...

A young farmer was filling out an application form for a job. When he came to the space for "remarks" he wrote— "Mighty Pretty Day. Hope you have one, too."

Reminder

Don't forget your lunch, keys, letters, money, cigarettes, cigars, snuff, chewing tobacco.

Last Words

Sayonara
    Adios
        Docvedanya
          Pip Pip